A Dog in a Hat

• • •

I had heard a lot of the old Belgians use the expression een hond met een hoed op, *which means "a dog with a hat on." In the context in which I heard it, I took it to mean that you see a dog in a hat when the normal situation changes, when something looks out of place.*

.

A Dog in a Hat

An American Bike Racer's Story of Mud, Drugs,
Blood, Betrayal, and Beauty in Belgium

○ ○ ○

Joe Parkin

BOULDER, COLORADO

1830 North 55th Street
Boulder, Colorado 80301-2700 USA
303/440-0601 · Fax 303/444-6788
E-mail velopress@insideinc.com

Distributed in the United States and Canada by Publishers Group West

Library of Congress Cataloging-in-Publication Data
Parkin, Joe.
A dog in a hat : an American bike racer's story of mud, drugs, blood, betrayal, and beauty in Belgium / Joe Parkin.
     p. cm.   ·
   ISBN 978-1-934030-26-4 (alk. paper)
1. Parkin, Joe.   2. Cyclists—Belgium—Biography.   3. Cyclists—United States—Biography.   4. Bicycle racing—Belgium—Biography.   5. Bicycle racing—United States—Biography. I.   Title.
GV1051.P37A3 2008
796.6—dc22
                    2008018544

For information on purchasing VeloPress books, please call 800/234-8356 or visit www.velopress.com.

Cover design by Andy Clymer
Cover illustration © Edel Rodriguez
Interior design by Anita Koury
Text is set in Prensa Book.

   09 10/ 10 9 8 7 6 5 4 3

To my mom, Nancy, who always understood dreams to be as important as reality and encouraged me to follow mine. And to her father, Ira, one of the most interesting people I ever knew, and perhaps part of the reason she was able to understand me.

Contents

Foreword

I DID TELL JOE PARKIN TO GO TO BELGIUM. I DID NOT, HOWEVER, tell him to stay.

But Joe stayed so long I began to wonder what the hell ever happened to him. Then about five years later I saw him coming toward me on the Schelde canal bike path. Now, you see a lot of cyclists on the canal, but there is no mistaking a profi for any of the beer-bellied supporters or even the desperado amateurs. The profis have an aloofness about their pedaling that shows true disdain for the wind, rain, or effort needed to propel themselves down the road. This rider approaching me at warp speed had all that in spades. He also had the emaciated skeletal silhouette many profis have. In fact, this dude was a wraith, with the gnarly skinny that only European pros possess. When the rider slowed and U-turned in front of me and said, "Oy, Bobke," I thought it was one of the spooky Flemish pros who had been pulverizing me for the majority of my adult life.

The rider said, *"Jongen, ik ben Joo."*

"Huh?" I said.

"Um" (long pause), "um" (longer pause). "It's Joe Parkin."

"Holy shit, don't lie!" I yelled. "Joe! Where have you been?"

"Hier . . . um . . . I've been here," said Joe.

"Whoa, dude, you scared me," I said.

After much chuckling, Joe explained in a rather cryptic mix of Flemish pro speak and half-remembered English that he was making a good living at kermesses, semiclassics, and smaller stage races.

I said, "Are you insane?"

Joe said, "Maybe," not even half joking.

At this stage in Joe's career, he was a true Vlaamse-man. Joe had gotten himself so deep into the fabric of the Flemish pro life, I feared he might not make it out. But as you can read in this vivid account of the hardships and triumphs of pro racing in Belgium, Joe not only survived but thrived in the toughest of all cycling environments. This is what I saw in Joe when we first met. And this is what I meant when I advised him to abandon the remedial form of four-square crit racing that prevailed in the States in the 1980s.

Joe was no longer the rheumatoid doughy tosser type that ruled Stateside racing in those days. He was an avenging angel of misery and, best of all, not a starry-eyed regional time trial champ with delusions of grandeur about to be sent home in a pain-induced coma after falling asleep in a crosswind battle. No, Joe knew the score. Joe had become the inside skinny. Joe was a twelve-toothed assassin.

What was it in those bleak landscapes that carved the fat off Joe's carcass like vultures around a kill? The weeks, months, and years of isolation in Belgium? The vicious, epic races that were virtually unknown by Americans then but are now part of our own cycling lore? The ancient, semi-illusionary dialect of a downtrodden people who revere cyclists as beacons of hope and cultural pride? The food, the dirty deals, the pig-shit toothpaste, the two-faced team managers, the smoky bars, homicidal teammates, and demented competitors? All these things and many more that you will read carved Joe into a missile of sinew, veins, sunken eyes, narrow shoulders, skinny arms, and huge ass and legs typical of a survivor of the toughest game on two wheels.

You should count yourself lucky to have stumbled across a treasure map from the old country of forgotten dreams and buried riches. In Belgium, bike racing rules, and I am not surprised in the least that Joe Parkin was a Flemish prince.

I have a rather ominous premonition that many a cycling fan will take umbrage with the grittier side of our sport that Joe writes about. If you do, you do not deserve to read this book— and feel free to FO and D! For everyone else, you may now read and be enlightened and entertained by the most authentic book ever written about making a two-wheeled living as a pro cyclist in Europe.

—*Bob Roll*

1

Nobody Else in the Photo

TELLING MY DAD THAT I WAS NOT GOING TO ANNAPOLIS OR ANY other military academy was one thing, since I had justified the decision immediately with the announcement that I was going to chase a U.S. Navy ROTC scholarship. Telling him that I was abandoning this latest goal in favor of a chance to race my bike was quite another. My announcement that I was going to put off college for the foreseeable future to race bicycles in Europe rendered him speechless.

Had it just been my dad, you would not be reading this now because more responsible minds would have prevailed, and I would surely have carted myself off to college, perhaps keeping the bike as an itching hobby. But my mom was there too, and she was my saving grace. My mom is an old soul who, while adhering to many of the strong beliefs and values of her and her parents' generations, sees life as something limited only by one's own imagination. I was born with a healthy dose of imagination, and

1

she always encouraged me to follow it. The announcement that silenced my dad brought only one dose of reality from my mom: "You're going to need another job," she said. "The one you have is not going to get you there."

I was an 18-year-old who was living at home while postponing college. I was working a couple of afternoons a week unpacking and assembling bikes at the California Pedaler, a local shop. Within a week of my mom's assessment, I was also working part-time at a frozen-yogurt shop and full-time at Burger King making $5.10 per hour. It was September 1985, and the racing season was more or less over. I figured, based largely upon what I read in *Fodor's* travel guide, that I would need to come up with an open-ended round-trip airline ticket and about $3,000. With that much money, I could probably live in a cheap hotel for three months.

I had gotten to know Bob Roll during the season; he lived close by and often hung out at the Pedaler. I'd had the opportunity to ride with him a few times and had seen him race some. From the giddyup, I knew I would like him. When I first met him, I had been in California for only a couple of weeks, and my repertoire of rides was pretty limited. I had just come off a ride up Mount Diablo with my training partner and tour guide, Carlos. We stopped by the Pedaler to see who might be hanging out there for Carlos to talk to.

As we rolled up to the shop, I saw a Basso bicycle leaning against the row of old movie-theater seats by the front door. It was a faded blue and bore the scratches of hard use. There was a sticker on it that indicated something Swiss, making it look even more formidable. Then I saw the tires. At first glance they looked like any other set of well-worn road tires, with the little black streaks all around that indicated they'd probably seen a rain shower or two. But as I got closer I noticed that there was actually writing on the sidewalls as well. The writing was hard to read; it seemed to have been written with a black ballpoint pen. But after a minute or so, I figured it out: "I was born in a crossfire hurricane. I was raised by a toothless biddy hag. . . ." The Rolling Stones lyrics continued. Before I could get to the next song, Bob had come out of the shop and was telling me I should trade my bike for his.

"There's pain and suffering in this bike," he said. "I need to have yours. It's brand new. You should give it to me."

At this point, my tour guide, Carlos, interrupted. "They call him Lobotomy Bob," he said. "His name is Bob Roll, and he's been racing in Europe. He's really fucking strong."

"Cool" was about all I could muster. Carlos, with his Puerto Rican accent and theatrical nature, introducing me to this strange guy in front of this bike shop that had once been a drive-through dairy store, made me feel like a kid who had just been taken to the freak show for the first time. I wasn't sure if I was in the presence of greatness or insanity, but I liked it somehow. I was still new to cycling, having only started racing a bike the summer before my senior year of high school. I'd gotten my racing license and won a couple of races in Minnesota, but I hadn't been quite sure I liked the riders all that much. Their overwhelming need for health and fairness over pure competition confused me. Bob was different. His bike, while clean, was beat to hell. It was a tool that he respected and cared for, but it did not sleep with him. Before I even had a chance to tell him that I planned on keeping my bike, he was back on his and rolling down the street.

● ● ●

3

I won the 1985 Sausalito Criterium in the Junior category, and Bob won the 1, 2, Pro race. I was having a good day and fairly dominated the race. Bob had just returned from the Giro d'Italia and was riding the local event with his Mug Root Beer team. It was the first year that the 7-Eleven team went to Europe as professionals and rode the Giro, and Bob was still in great shape. He simply destroyed his race. I had had some good races and had received numerous offers to race with the bigger regional teams for the following season, but Bob set me straight.

"Don't do it," he warned. "Don't ride with these guys. Go to Belgium."

It was probably that night or the night after when I made the announcement to my parents and started making preparations. As luck would have it, there was no international racing (or not much of it) in Belgium until June 1. At that point, all of the small races would open to riders from any part of the world. So the fact that I was working ten hours a day and not really training was not such a big deal.

Nor was it a problem that I would not have the money I needed until the end of March. Bob had given me two names and addresses in Belgium. I wrote two or three letters to Albert Claeys, telling him that I was a friend of Bob Roll, who had recommended that I contact him, and asking if I might be able to rent a room from him. Bob had told me Albert was probably my best opportunity in Belgium because he had been working as a mechanic for the 7-Eleven team in Europe and liked Americans enough that having a young American amateur stay with him and his family might be okay. I never got a response.

On April 10, 1986, I packed as much stuff as I could into a large hockey bag, loaded my bike and a spare set of wheels into a green nylon bike bag, and took off for the San Francisco airport with my dad. My mom was recovering from surgery, and I had said my good-byes to her earlier that day.

Neither my dad nor I had much to say on the ride to the airport. I was too caught up in the task at hand, and my dad, I later found out from a letter he wrote, was sad to see me go. We allowed a little more time than normal to get me checked in. This flight was taking place in the wake of some terrorist activities, so my dad, who had planned on accompanying me to my departure gate, was not allowed past the security check. While I know now that he wished he could walk me right onto the plane, holding my hand the whole time, I think it was easier on me to have him stopped there. He paused for a minute and then gave me his ultimate offering of respect as he reached out his hand instead of hugging me. It was the handshake he would have offered a colleague.

● ● ●

Fourteen hours later, I was in Brussels, totally worn out. I collected my two bags and made my way through customs. We had been told that because of the terrorist activity, we should get out of the airport as quickly as possible. I made my way to the information desk and was greeted by one of the most beautiful women I ever saw in Belgium. It's quite possible that I was seeing her through jet-lag goggles. Or I may just have been shocked that she was not one of the typically frumpy, sometimes angry help-desk people you see in the States. She was, in fact, awake and alert, with long black hair, and, I realized some time later, was very tan for a Belgian.

She gave me directions, and I humped the ever-increasing weight of my two bags to the train platform. I took the train from Zaventem, the Brussels airport, to the central station. There I boarded a train for Gent and sat in a car that was empty except for one other guy, who was probably a year or two older than I. After a few minutes the conductor came on board and punched my ticket. He and the other guy started arguing in a language that I imagined to be Russian. It occurred to me that it was unlikely that two people on a train in Belgium who didn't know each other would be speaking Russian, but the language sounded so strange to me that I couldn't be sure. I knew that this part of Belgium spoke Flemish, a language I had always believed to be a derivative of French with some German thrown in for good measure. I thought Flemish would sound a lot more like French (which I had studied in school) than this Russian-sounding exchange I was listening to. The argument seemed heated and culminated with the conductor kicking at the guy's feet for some reason.

I got my stuff off the train at Gent's central station and sat for a few minutes on a bench. It was just after noon, and I was tired. My original plan had been to call Mr. Claeys once I'd arrived in Gent, but I was too tired; I'd never make it that far. I felt weak and worthless and just wanted to sleep. I decided the best thing to do would be to find a hotel and get some rest.

Each few steps forward with the two big bags on my shoulders felt like a mile, so I had to stop frequently and rest. In fifteen minutes I made it the whole hundred feet from the bench where I had been sitting to the front of the station. Off to my right I saw what looked like a row of small hotels. Many minutes and several rest stops later, I was in front of the first hotel in the row. I stared at it for a minute and then moved to the next one. By the third or fourth hotel, I saw several country flags and the appropriate word for "rooms" by each respective flag. I set my bags down and entered the hotel. After I handed over 750 francs (about $17 at that time), I was given a large metal key fob with an old-fashioned key attached. I found my way to the room and didn't get out of bed until about 11 the next morning. Four hours and one phone call later, I was in Ursel on the doorstep of Albert Claeys.

○ ○ ○

It's fitting in many ways that my first task as a European cyclist was a trip to the doctor. This was long before anybody was talking about drugs in cycling, or at least long before the mainstream media knew about it. Cyclists were talking to each other, and the rumors brought back by Americans who had ventured abroad were horror stories. Ever since I had announced I was going to go to Belgium to give racing a try, I'd been collecting drug warnings like bad pennies. From Nancy Reagan to the guys I had raced against as juniors the year before to the coked-up mechanics at the shop where I hung out and pretended to turn wrenches, everybody was telling me to "just say no."

My arrival in Ursel could not have been more perfect. It was raining, and there were bike races going on. In my mind, rain, cobblestones, and bike races equal Belgium, then as now. Maybe seeing the country for the first time exactly as I had imagined it helped seal the deal. It was my goal to become a professional cyclist—a Belgian cyclist. I was willing to do almost whatever it took to achieve that goal. Normally a trip to the doctor was something I'd undertake only in an emergency, but my new coach, Albert, insisted. Albert had been around cycling for several years.

7

He was the son of a pre–World War II champion of Flanders who had won a stage at the Giro d'Italia. He had also been a mechanic for some of the bigger Belgian teams of the '70s and '80s. He told me I had to go to the doctor to be tested because, after all, one could not make a racehorse out of a jackass. If the numbers were not good, he would send me packing.

I didn't even ride my bike before I went to the doctor. We headed off to the appointment, and it was one of the longest forty-five-minute car rides of my life. Despite the fact that I was enjoying the surroundings, the food, and the coffee, I was terrified. I have been arrested on two continents and deported from one country; I have crashed cars, bicycles, motorcycles, and an airplane. But none of these traumatic experiences compares with the sheer horror of this doctor visit.

Given the pass/fail nature of the visit, you'd think I would have been afraid of the results, but that wasn't the problem. Instead, I was stuck on a ghoulish vision of doctors and their evil syringes bent on stealing the innocence of pure-hearted American cyclists. Seriously, you'd have thought my 148 pounds of shaved-legged youth had just been put on the bus to San Quentin. I was scared to death. The office itself was amazing; it had a collection of equipment that to my 19-year-old mind was more suited to an antiques collection than a doctor's office. The presiding doctors were a father-and-son team, specializing in sports medicine. True to form, they poked and prodded and asked many questions. Their hands were cold and their sense of humor absent. They could easily have been mistaken for cheap caricatures of themselves. I was a perfect patient, lest they harvest my brains. I was asked to lie on an examining table. Though it was not cold, I found myself shaking like a leaf, as I thought this was where the needles would come out and the soul-stealing would begin. The senior doctor hooked some leather straps to my wrists and ankles, each with wires connected to a tan steel box. Incredibly, I did not die and no magic potion was injected into my veins, but my trembling didn't stop. Dr. Leinders said something to the other two, who began to laugh and then translated for me that he was chiding himself for having cold hands. It was a nice gesture, but not enough for me to let my guard down.

It was amazing how accurately the doctors' numbers foretold the truth. The rest of the tests that day had to do with how well I would perform as a cyclist for the rest of my career. The good doctors had compiled quite a bit of data on riders and had devised a graph that would put me into a category of cyclist. At the bottom of the list was "Cyclo-tourist" and "Amateur" and then a boundary line signifying "Beroepsrenner" (professional). At the lower end of the professional category was the "Kermis racer" and then "Classics racer," with the top level being "Tour winner." I fell into the category of classics riders, somewhere in the middle of that group.

Had I really understood the significance of the tests (that is, had I been a real Belgian), I would probably have made a lot more money in the sport than I did. If I had grasped the significance of the numbers and been raised in a culture that values a rider finishing alone, his clothing covered in pig shit, as much as one finishing with a celebratory group wearing yellow, things would have been different. I would probably have given up the polka-dotted dream I'd carried with me to Europe, settled into the life of a solid classics journeyman, and reaped the rewards available in Belgium to a pro of that stature. I most definitely would not have stood on the scale three times a day to keep my weight down to that magical, below-70-kilograms (154 pounds) mark I needed to maintain if I were going to transform myself into the king of the mountains. I am sure I would have learned how to sprint better. One of the truly beautiful things about cycling, however, is the fact that there is no such thing as 20/20 hindsight because there are too many variables. If I had understood and accepted the verdict of the numbers, I might not have given it the shot I gave it. Who knows?

● ● ●

Less than a year later, I was an established Belgian amateur cyclist with several wins to my name. I had placed third in the amateur version of the Het Volk Classic while riding for a local Belgian club. This in itself was amazing because Americans were not allowed on Belgian club teams unless they had official residence in the country. The chicanery that got me into amateur classics in 1987 would have amazed even Johnny Cochran, but incredibly, nobody asked any questions. I was being courted by the pros now. This was the era of Greg LeMond, after all, and an American who could actually pedal a bike through the wind, rain, and cold and understand the native language projected an aura of dollar signs wherever he went.

In Belgium, a good local amateur is like an all-state high school quarterback in Texas. A decent local pro has about the same value as the amateur but lacks the promise of greatness in the future. I was a good amateur who held the American card. I was like the actor who goes after a rock-star fantasy—everyone wants to be there when you rise to the top, but they are just as happy to see you fail miserably.

The main source of income for the Claeys family came from the café Albert and his wife Rita, ran together. It occupied most of the ground floor of the house and was connected to the kitchen where we had our meals. I liked to hang out in the café for as long as I could handle the smoke, and I got to know the regulars pretty well. Before each race I was given advice from any number of local drunks. I was constantly reminded of what to do, what to look for, and what to eat—and above all reminded that I must win. After the race, if I had done well, the beer flowed like a river in the café and the race would be replayed until the last supporter stumbled out to his car, usually in the wee hours of the morning. If the race had not gone well, the story would be entirely different. If I'd managed to screw up, only the most hardcore supporters would come back to the café. There'd be only a couple of these, but they would hang on, getting more and more ornery, outlasting the rest of the customers through sheer anger. It would take almost as long on these bad nights to get the café closed up, but the money brought in would be less by a long shot.

○ ○ ○

I liked the fact that the pros were looking at me. I had come to Belgium to become one, after all. Albert didn't agree. He felt that I was young enough to give the Olympics a shot before turning pro. The 1988 Summer Olympics in Seoul, South Korea, were quickly approaching, and I was riding well. To get on the U.S. Olympic team, I'd have to be approved by American cycling's governing body, the United States Cycling Federation (USCF), so I started petitioning the USCF coaches for a spot on the National B Team for the amateur Tour of Belgium. That seemed to me to be the best way to get my foot in the USCF's door. But after numerous attempts and a few hundred dollars' worth of international phone calls, I gave up. I was told that it did not matter what races I had ridden or won; if I wanted to be considered for any U.S. team, I had to return to the States and ride the prescribed course of selection races. Although I felt (and still feel) that this reasoning was idiotic, I was relieved and happy that there was no further reason for me to race as an amateur. I would now be able to get on with what I had set out to do in the first place.

To this day, I have a hard time speaking cycling like an American. I cut my teeth racing in Belgium, so its expressions are the ones that come naturally to me. I think the most beautiful one is "nobody else in the photo," which is the ultimate way to win a race—so far ahead of second place that the only rider pictured in the sports section the next day is the guy who won. My last race as an amateur took place on a circuit nearly identical to the one used for the time trial in the Three Days of de Panne. It was a course that would kick the living hell out of me as a pro, but for this last event as an amateur, it allowed me to finish minutes ahead of second place. There was nobody else in the photo. I signed my first professional cycling contract on July 4, 1987.

● ● ●

With my new Transvemij jersey on my back and my new U.S. Pro Cycling Federation (USPRO) racing license in hand, I headed to a professional kermis race to try out my legs. In many cases the team director will make these races mandatory, but for this race I was on my own. There was another race going on elsewhere, so I didn't expect to see many other Transvemij riders show up.

In Belgium it is illegal to get dressed for a race in or around your car. Amateur racers often knock on doors to find garage space to use as dressing rooms. Pros usually have it better. Either they are invited into the back courtyard of a café or restaurant or they will find themselves in the living room of one of the houses lining the start/finish straight. If you find yourself in one of these houses, it's because you have been brought there as the guest of another pro, and you'll be obliged to go back to that same place year after year. A friend of Albert, a rider by the name of Patrick Versluys, invited me to come along to some old lady's kitchen about 20 yards from the start line. There were two other racers there as well.

The routine for getting ready for a kermis race is painfully comical. Typically the rider will sit down and place a small bath towel in front of the chair for his feet. He'll then start pinning on his number. Once he's made sure all of the pins are pointing the same direction, he'll take off his shirt and start taking inventory of his race gear. He'll probably sit until twenty-five minutes before the start before getting dressed the rest of the way. Whether or not he plans on being "good" for the race, he will not leave for the start line until ten minutes or less before the gun.

In those days, if a rider planned on being "good" for the race, then exactly fifteen minutes before the start a syringe would come out. Some clear liquid would be sucked up into it from any number of different ampoules and injected, either subcutaneously or intravenously. If injected subcutaneously, the substance was usually a low-grade amphetamine. Injecting it this way would create little time-release lumps under the skin that the riders called *"bolleketten,"* which basically means "little rocket balls." Depending on the length of the race and/or its importance, a rider might have as many as four of these little balls hidden under the sleeves of his jersey or legs of his shorts. The shoulder area was the typical spot, since that was an area that might still have some fat on it. If the amphetamines were surgical-quality, the rider would probably shoot them directly into the "canal." There are plenty of medical preparations that have genuine, legal uses for a cyclist, but as a general rule, anything being shot fifteen minutes before the start of a lesser race can be considered suspect.

Of all the strange stuff I got to see during my career as a racer, one of the strangest was something I saw before that first kermis. One of the guys in the kitchen, a third-year Dutch pro, started getting ready on a slightly different schedule than what I would come to recognize as normal. Versluys and I entered the kitchen about an hour before the race was to start, and the two others had just gotten themselves situated when we walked in. I had not even gotten the first pin pushed into my number when the Dutch guy started filling a 1-cc syringe with clear liquid from a 10-cc *"potje."* Satisfied with the amount, he poked the needle into a little tent of skin on his arm and shot it. Ten seconds later he started giggling like a four-year-old and pointed to the hair on the arm he'd injected. *"Kijk kijk kijk kijk,"* he said, in between giggles. He was apparently hoping we'd enjoy the sight of hair standing on end as much as he did. Five minutes later he did it again, and then again, and again after that. After each injection, he was equally amazed.

The other two laughed at the show each time. I couldn't laugh. I wasn't scared, really; I think I was more shocked than anything else. I had been warned that it would be weird here in the big time. Some time before, when it had begun to look like I might have a chance of getting a contract, I had often been told that a couple

of years in the pros made one crazy. After each of these warnings, I smiled and nodded dutifully, not understanding whether
it was supposed to be the drugs or the culture of the professional
peloton that would make one crazy. In retrospect, I think it is
probably a combination of the two and dependent on how deeply
a rider gets into each.

I was 11th in the race. I attacked out of a big group with about
2 km to go, and surprisingly, I was not caught.

○ ○ ○

Jules de Wever was the first *sportdirekteur* I'd know in the pro
ranks. Jules had done a long stint with the famous Ti Raleigh
team in Holland alongside Peter Post. He was now the boss of the
two-year-old Transvemij/Van Schilt team, which would become
known as TVM in the following years. The team was, honestly,
mostly a collection of worn-out veterans and rookies, with a few
kermis racers thrown in just to add to the discord. I doubt that it
would be possible to put together a more dysfunctional group of
people. The veterans disliked the rookies. The Dutch hated the
Belgians. The Dutch hated me. The Belgians distrusted the Dutch.
Nobody had much respect for the kermis racers. Nobody but, I
think, Jos Lammertink and I had any respect for Jules.

Throw together any group of highly motivated, highly competitive, and sometimes chemically altered athletes, and tensions
will mount—but this was terrible. I'd grown up listening to my
father's stories about being a drill instructor in the U.S. Marine
Corps. I had been the new kid in eleven different schools before
getting my high school diploma. I fully expected to get hassled
for being a rookie and maybe a little more for being an American.

15

But what I encountered on this team was ridiculous. It was so full of holes and factions that no teamwork was ever accomplished. Despite the fact that I was in the same room getting dressed with the rest of the team when Jules introduced me, I was still asked repeatedly throughout the race who I was and what I thought I was doing. When I tried to get to the front of the field to help out our teammate and local favorite, Jan Bogaert, I was told to get back and stay out of the way—by another member of the Transvemij squad. Bogaert, a Belgian sprinter and kermis specialist, won the first race I entered with the rest of the team. He won it by himself, with a little help from Jos Lammertink.

About a week later we shipped off to Burgos, Spain, for a week-long stage race in the hills. The race started with a short prologue, followed the next day by a 125-kilometer (km) stage in the morning and a 22-km team time trial in the afternoon. I had been neither the best nor the worst on the team for the first two stages. I was scared about the team time trial; I had never done one before, and the Dutch are specialists at the race. About two hours before the start, the team's head soigneur showed up in my room and placed two suppositories, one for my roommate and one for me, on the windowsill. I had bought a couple of American magazines in the airport on my way down and spent the next hour staring at the pictures. My teammate fell asleep. As we got ready to go racing, my teammate noticed the suppos had melted. He scraped what he could off the windowsill, but I left mine right where it was. Set aside the fact that I was still trying to pay attention to what Nancy Reagan and the others had to say, there was no way I was shoving anything up my butt—let alone some sort of melted goo complete with Spanish windowsill particles—for a kind of race I had never done before.

I was the first one dropped. I don't think it had anything to do with the suppository. I think it was the fact that I was supposed to get dropped. In the years since, I have done several team time trials and have learned how the game is played. If they want you gone, you're gone. It is quite easy, in fact. The bulk of the team simply holds the rider in question out on the front a little too long before coming over the top of him so that he can rest for his next turn on the front. As soon as he is clear of that lead bike position, the rest of the team accelerates so hard that they snap past him as he comes through to grab the last wheel position. A little gap will form, one that he has to close quickly. By the time he is firmly planted back on the wheel in front of him, all of the other riders have done a half turn and his nose is stuck back out into the wind again.

I lasted just three turns and was gone. By the time we reached the finish line, four other Transvemij riders had joined me dangling off the back. The survivors weren't even in the top five. Two days later, I climbed into the number-two team car halfway through the stage and gave my number to a race official. Before the prologue I had weighed 70 kilos (154 pounds). After four days in Spain, I weighed just 62 (137 pounds). Welcome to the pros.

● ● ●

It was late in the season of my first half-year as a professional cyclist when I got the call from Jules that I'd be doing the Paris-Brussels fall classic. I was excited—Paris-Brussels was, after all, a real classic, complete with big teams and fast riders—but I was also a little shocked. Paris-Brussels has always been considered a sprinter's race, and although I have been called a lot of things over the years, "sprinter" has never been one of them. Jules told me that I had been riding well; I just needed to figure out when and how things happened in the pro peloton.

Although Jules de Wever was indeed giving me an opportunity to go learn in a big race, I think he was also sticking me in there to get back at the owner of the team. Jules was not going to be the number-one director for the next year. Cees Priem, who was currently pedaling out his final days as a bike rider, would be taking the reins in 1988. Jules could stay on if he wanted, but there was no way he would let himself be relegated to driving in the kermis caravan. Besides, I don't think Cees had much respect for the old man. Priem was, after all, a tall Dutch rider with a résumé, and De Wever was a small Belgian director who had not done much with the mixed band of idiots he'd been commanding.

I hated Cees Priem. I still do. Less than a week after we returned from Burgos, Jules called to tell me I had to race a kermis race somewhere in East Flanders. He had watched me race in Spain, of course, so he knew I was not exactly 100 percent, but he told me I had to go. The team had gotten a contract with the race organizer, and we needed a certain minimum number of riders on the line or there would be no start money for its director.

Jules told me to stay in the race until the halfway point and then go home. I have dropped out of a lot of races over the years. Sometimes I dropped out because the training plan called for half a race. Other times I just did not feel like racing that day. But I was still a sparkly fresh rookie at this point, and the thought of bailing out of a perfectly good bike race was not part of my vocabulary. On the other hand, I was still physically and mentally beat from my less-than-stellar pro stage race debut, so going home after a few laps sounded like a great plan.

We had just gone through the start/finish line for the go-home lap minus one when I heard Cees Priem yelling at me: "What are you doing back here? You must be at the front. Your job is to be at the front." I had to look back over my right shoulder to about 5 o'clock to find him. I was trying to process the fact that some dude I didn't know was yelling at me from behind to go ride at the front. We were hardly even in the same time zone as the front of the peloton.

"Eh?" I barked. When in doubt, respond with a questioning noise in at least a similar dialect to the region in which you're racing. It didn't work.

"You must be racing at the front. You are a young boy," was his clarification.

"I'm sick. I was in Burgos, and I got sick. Jules said I must only start," I said and then repeated myself in Flemish. *"Ik ben ik ziek. Ik heb in Burgos geweest. Jules zegt dat ik moet alleen de start nemen."*

It didn't matter. According to Cees, I was worthless and should go to the front.

I endured the verbal flogging for the rest of the lap, and then about forty of us peeled off the back of the peloton and down a hidden alley a few hundred yards before the start/finish line. Cees Priem was there too; so much for leading by example. I began the process of getting out of my contract with TVM for the 1988 season.

○ ○ ○

When you learn to fly, people constantly tell you about your first solo: the moment when your instructor steps out of the plane to let you take off and land by yourself. Your first solo is supposedly the most magical experience in your flying career. However, I did not see real flying magic until the first time I flipped the airplane upside down. That magic was amazing! Similarly, I am not sure I noticed I was a real pro until I was lined up at the start of Paris-Brussels.

At that point in my months-old career, I had already been beaten up by the press, drug-tested, dropped by my own team-mates, fined for hanging on to a team car (at 120 kilometers per hour[kph]), bunged up by crashing into a drunk while chasing after a 200-Belgian-franc prime (less than $5 at that time), and yelled at more times than I can remember just for being a rookie. But standing on the start line of Paris-Brussels I was a real pro bike racer, with my name printed in the official program and everything. It was a late-season classic that I had no chance of winning. I was riding for a second-rate team in an also-ran classic. I had no hero card and no favored-to-win teammate. Still, I felt I had made it to the big league.

In the late 1980s, if a rider did not have a great palmarès, he had to have a great presence on television. In other words, you could get away without any results as long as you could find your way to the front of the peloton and in front of the cameras when the race went live. Therefore, when the Eurovision helicopter flew over the race with two hours to go, the shit hit the fan. Riders you'd never seen before were now ready to run you off the road for the chance to show their team jersey and sponsor's logo on European television for even a second or two.

Paris-Brussels was a long race that year, 310 km. I do not remember even getting into the big chainring until we got close to the Belgian border. The slow tempo created a false sense of security because I wasn't ready for the tempo to lift when it did.

From the Belgian border until just 40 km to go, I don't think I shifted. I did look back a couple of times just to make sure there were no more gears to use. There never were.

Between 40 km and 20 km to go, there were some changes. The chaff had been weeded out for the most part, and the favorites took time to pee, eat a little bit more, and size each other up for the final push, all the while holding an average of close to 50 kph. At 20 km to go, Sean Kelly moved to the back of the peloton to pee one last time. Two of his KAS teammates hung back with him, one of them pushing him along. That was the moment when I knew I had made it. There was 20 km to go, and the Irish great Sean Kelly had just forced a little reprieve.

I had been eating and drinking pretty well throughout the day, and my gut was distended like that of one of those famine children on TV. Still, I ate some more warm, mushy crap from my back tight pockets and washed it down with lukewarm tea. Then I ditched everything except one bottle. I cannot remember anything after that until the sign indicating that I had 10 km to go.

At that moment, the man with the hammer came to visit. A bike racer, especially a rookie in his first big classic, fears the man with the hammer as much as the grim reaper. The man with the hammer beat the living hell out of me—all at once—and the peloton rode away from me with 10 km to go.

Even though I was now riding alone, I just needed to hang on for another 10 minutes, and my first classic finale would have been in the record books. I settled for simply finishing my first classic and opted for survival-mode pedaling. Nope . . . too fast. I slowed down again. I looked back to see the bus behind me. Every big point-to-point race has a bus that collects the dead, and at 300 of 310 km, this bus was full of sweaty, stinky, impatient losers wanting to hurry up and get it over with. The last thing I wanted to do in the whole world was to get on that bus. Who can't pedal a bike 10 km anyway?

I'm not sure what the exact distance to go was because there were no signs. Suffice it to say that after 300-something of 310 km, the flesh was no longer willing to humor the spirit. I had to climb into the bus. At 200 km, we had been almost an hour behind schedule. Wim Arras crossed the line at 8 hours and 24 minutes to win the race. Four years later he would be turning wrenches on my bike.

2

Langst de Vaart

IF I COULD RELIVE ONE PERIOD OF THE PAST, IT WOULD BE MY FIRST full season as a pro, in 1988. It was by no means the greatest year of my life, or of my career—but it was pivotal, and it was fascinating. I was starting to gain some wisdom as a racer but had absolutely no road-weariness yet. I was still learning what the hell I was doing and consequently made way too many rookie mistakes.

The writing seemed to be stenciled on the wall at the TVM camp at the end of the 1987 season. I had been given a contract that was valid for seventeen and a half months and had used up only about three. But with Jules out and Mr. Priem in, I figured I was not going to be a happy soldier if I had to stay. Albert and I talked about it with Jules and made the decision to make a run for it. I exercised my right to get out of a contract, breaking all ties to TVM for the 1988 season. In reality, Cees Priem and the folks at the insurance company (Transvemij, later TVM, is a freight insurance company) were most likely happy with my request.

A DOG IN A HAT

Jules still thought I showed promise, but my results so far didn't really speak to it.

If there's a universal truth in cycling, it's that team owners and directors are always on the verge of "the biggest deal ever." I have had the privilege of riding for quite a few directors, and they all dream of that one big sponsor to come along. They dream it so hard that they believe it, and then, with all the zeal of an evangelical minister in the Southern United States, they sell the dream to the rider. In the end the directors are there to sell: They have to sell the rider on the idea of bringing out that one more little effort; they even have to sell the rider on the idea of riding with the team in the first place. In fact, it is their job to get the absolute most out of the rider at all times. When a directeur sportif you have read about in the local papers, seen on TV, and maybe even read about in American cycling magazines tells you he thinks you should come with him to a new team because you have talent, you keep listening. When he follows up with a promise that you'll be able to ride all of the classics, lots of little stage races, and one of the Grand Tours, you look for a pen.

At that point in my career, I believed I could be the next Lucien van Impe. I had already figured out that my chances of ever wearing yellow in Paris were slim, but I was still holding on to my dream of wearing the polka dots there. I also wanted a chance to do the small stage races in Italy, Spain, and France. Jules was going to team up with Florent van Vaerenberg, bringing his new sponsor to Florent's team. Both directors had long and colorful histories, and both were willing to give me a shot. In 1987 Florent had directed the Lucas/Atlanta/Garcia squad, based in Belgium. It was a second-rate team, really, with several guys who didn't belong in the pro ranks and one, Bjarne Riis, who at the time didn't seem to me to be pro material, but who would win the Tour de France a few years later. I did not feel all that good about my soon-to-be teammates, but Florent had some substantial contacts in Spain and promised me lots of little, hilly stage races. I loved the little stage races. I signed up.

I returned from the States a little fatter than I should have been, but I was nonetheless ready to go. The team, however, was not. There had been sponsor problems, and what had seemed to be a sure thing a few weeks earlier was now sketchy at best. Riis had already escaped to join Toshiba, and the rest of the lineup was looking shaky too. I didn't know what to do. It was just after the first of the year and by my way of thinking way too late to be dealing with this sort of dilemma.

I called Jim Ochowicz, who was the general manager of the American 7-Eleven team, to tell him what was going on with my deal. In early 1987, when I was still an amateur, Och had given me a 7-Eleven team bike. It was the only piece of equipment I ever got as an amateur without actually having to fork out any cash. We had made a verbal deal at the time that I would be available to turn pro with 7-Eleven should they need me.

Times were different back then. Today riders make decent money, and American cyclists who go to Europe look at it as the place to be, the final destination, as opposed to the "crash course in fast" that they considered it then. Many of the 7-Eleven team riders were good criterium riders in the United States who could make thousands of dollars every week in those 60- to 90-minute races. Perhaps the American-based sponsor demanded participation in a certain number of events. Perhaps the guys got homesick for races where they could understand the announcer and where they were treated as big stars. Or perhaps they just got sick of

Belgium and its gray skies. Whatever the reason, the American riders on the 7-Eleven team often headed home after a very short period, leaving holes in the roster that had to be filled. Och had hired several English-speaking riders, convincing them to turn pro and race with the team. These guys were already living in Belgium, trying to make it to the pros, so the bonus of equipment and entry in races they only dreamed of was good enough.

I told Och that, at least for the moment, I was out of a job. It took him a few days, but he agreed to hire me. There was a catch, though. If I wanted to be a 7-Eleven rider, I had to sign a contract good for only five months and accept a $500-per-month salary.

To say I felt as if I had just been punched in the gut doesn't quite describe my reaction to his offer. I wasn't angry, but I didn't feel like thanking him profusely either. I was relieved to have been offered a shot at the big American team and to have the option of continuing my career, but I couldn't figure out how the whole thing would work financially. If there had been a guarantee or at least a casual assurance that I'd be racing all the time, the money part would have been bearable. I knew this would not be the case, though, since the big American riders on the squad would be coming and going in and out of the roster. My schedule would be about as sure as a first-year substitute teacher's.

The short term of the contract was a problem too. I was still a young and relatively inexperienced rider who had not proved himself to the boss. If I limped through the classics or got hurt somehow, the dream would have ended with no chance at redemption in the late-season races. The Transvemij contract I had recently killed had been worth almost three times as much per month and been good for a full twelve months. I was starting to regret my decision to jump ship.

As I turned the problem over in my mind, I concluded that I was going to have to call Och back and take the job. I had been vacillating between visions of the worst-case scenario—getting dropped in the classics without even so much as helping one of the team leaders do something important—and the best-case scenario—being a hero of the 7-Eleven team, finishing all of the classics with the top group. At almost the very minute my imagination peaked atop one of the good waves, the phone rang. Florent had gotten a sponsor, Eurotop, and the contract I had traded was now good.

I should have been elated by the news, but I wasn't. I had been soft-pedaling my training, questioning the point of suffering the end of winter in Belgium. I was pleased that I would now have an answer to the question my body would ask when I had to put the screws to it, but that was where the satisfaction I gained from Florent's call ended. Of course I could have gotten out of it if I'd really wanted to roll the dice with 7-Eleven. But it was the best available deal. I decided to stick it out.

That was when I met Cocquyt.

If the only thing I was able to take away from my Belgian experience was my friendship with Patrick Cocquyt, I would still be lucky. In many ways, I think the reason I relate so well to the Belgians—even picture myself somewhat a Belg—is because of the time I spent with Cocquyt *langst de vaart,* or along the canal. That was the way it all started.

With the announcement that this shitkicker-cum-world-beater-cum-not-yet-finalized team was actually a reality, I hooked up with my soon-to-be new teammate Patrick Cocquyt for some training rides. In my mind he was already in the big time, having been a member of the Hitachi squad a couple of years before. When he contacted Albert to schedule some training rides

27

with me, I was more than anxious to get things going. This was to be my first full year as a pro, after all, so the bigger the jump I could get, the better.

In 1988, there were no power meters to measure your output in watts, and even the heart rate monitors people were using were misunderstood. Instead we trained with hours and with gearing. My gear of choice was a 42x15 or 16. It was a good gear for the early season, or so I thought. I could do my little rides sitting on the back of my saddle and watch my Avocet computer; 30–32 kph was my number. I had about six different rides, each of which ended on the half hour, with the longest being two and a half hours. I got to race so much that I didn't feel the need to do long training.

Cocquyt's program was a little different. He had a thing for the five-hour ride, and his gear of choice was the 52x16. Our pace was about the same; we just looked different. Cocquyt's bike was perfectly Belgian, with shallow, criterium-style handlebars covered in padded white vinyl tape. The bike itself had been washed so many times that there seemed to be wear marks from the various sponges and brushes used to clean it. There was black gunk encrusted in the parts of the bike that sponges and brushes and diesel fuel would not clean. The saddle was perfectly broken in, like a baseball glove you might find at an estate sale, some of the leather being darker and greasier, and of course both sides of it were torn at the back, evidence of at least one crash on either side. It was not uncommon for the Belgians of that era to ride the same saddle for more than one year.

His position on the bike was cool too. He sat fairly upright with an arched back. His legs never seemed to straighten, and his knees bowed out. Most riders seem to have some ankle movement during the pedal stroke, but Cocquyt's feet never changed from the same flat plane. His very demeanor on the bicycle was uncanny, as if he were a TV gangster who had been accidentally dressed in Lycra and dropped onto a bike. I have no doubt that had he been born in the United States and given a guitar at the same age he'd been given a racing bicycle in Belgium, Cocquyt would be a zillionaire.

Our first training ride together began as they all would: 8:45, *langst de vaart*. That meant I would have to leave at about 8:15 and he would have to leave at 8:30. We would be riding from opposite ends of the path, so would eventually meet up with each other. Albert told me that we would be riding about five hours, so I left the house equipped with bottles and food. Typically, in the 1980s, Europeans rode with one bottle and attached two only if they were about to compete in one of the Grand Tours or a classic. American riders always had two water-bottle cages attached, and my bike was no different. Cocquyt's and my first conversation was about carrying water bottles.

"Are you planning on going far?" he asked in his thick dialect that was a combination of Gentse and other flat Flemish inflections.

"I don't know," I responded. "Albert said we would be riding about five hours, so I have bottles."

"Bottles are only for racing," he told me. "I don't think we will ever get too far away from a place where we can get a Coke if we become thirsty."

I was sold. I bought into the Patrick Cocquyt philosophy instantly. This was a belief shared by most of the Belgian pros of the era and certainly makes sense if you consider the fact that most of them find cycling as an escape from revolving-shift factory work.

29

When you get hungry, you stop the work at hand, sit down, and enjoy some nourishment.

Cocquyt and I rode the same 125-km route most of the time. At its farthest point, it took us all the way to Ronse, where the 1988 World Championship was to be held. We figured out the best bakery along the way for each type of cake. For a young pro bike racer, there were often fringe benefits at the various delicious bakeries that are found in every town. You will almost always find these bakeries staffed by the wife or daughter of the baker. If it is the wife behind the pastry case, you have two chances: Either she is old and fat, or she is young and pretty. In the latter case, there is a good chance that the young wife has not spoken more than two words to her husband in weeks because they are on different schedules. Of course this worked out well for us, as there was a strong possibility that one of us would be invited back for "tea."

Side by side for five hours a day is a lot of time to spend with another person, but we just kept having more fun as time rolled on. Cocquyt exuded the cockiness of a Triple-A baseball player and the dry, quick wit to back it up. His digs came in slowed-down, midcentury gangster-movie chirps that often made me wonder what James Cagney would have looked like riding a bicycle. No one was immune either: other riders, soigneurs, mechanics, directors, innocent bystanders—everyone was fair game.

He liked to stop with about two hours to go in the ride and have a Coke. They were always pulled off a shelf and thus were never cold. Drinking a Coke that's at room temperature takes a little getting used to and even then cannot be done quickly. If it was not raining we would lean on the bikes and enjoy the passing traffic. Belgians know about bike racing, and they knew we were pros even if they did not know us by name. Most people would nod at us and say hello, sometimes adding good-luck wishes. But as it goes with any major spectator sport, a little bit of knowledge can be a very dangerous thing, and some people thought it more fitting to give us grief. Once we were sitting outside Madame Ananas's little grocery store (we called her this because her hairdo made her head look like a giant pineapple). Out of nowhere one of the locals berated us for taking a break.

"You'll never win the Ronde sitting there drinking Coke," he accused.

I wasn't sure if he was talking about the Ronde van Vlaanderen or the Ronde van Frankrijk. None of that mattered to Cocquyt, though. Calmly and without even lifting his head, he responded, "Maybe not, but Coke makes me aggressive and as soon as I finish I should be good enough to pound your face in." He paused for a second and looked up at the man, who clearly was having a hard time processing what he'd just heard. "Asshole." The man turned and walked away.

"You see, Joe? These people would just as soon knock you off your bike with their welfare cards. It's always the same."

With that I began to wonder what it was really like to be a Belgian bike racer. I would feel it more as the years went on, as I learned to think and speak the language and breathe the culture. The Belgian people are very much fair-weather fans, and that attitude is compounded by the fact that their biggest national hero was the greatest cyclist of all time, Eddy Merckx. For every generation to follow him, Merckx will forever be the measure of a cyclist, albeit one that is out of reach. No young Belgian boy can climb onto a tricycle without being cast in Merckx's shadow. It's a huge shadow, and one that has surely affected the careers of some notable bike riders.

● ● ●

Late winter was rolling into early spring, and despite Cocquyt's company, I was getting bored with training. Belgium was good for me because I was never a good trainer. I liked to race—the more races the better. Early season is not good for this because there are too few kermis races. Our little team had neither the budget nor the clout to get into the season-preparatory stage races in the south of France, Italy, and Spain, so we would be going into the classics season cold. Lucky for me, I had no idea how much pain and suffering this was soon going to cause.

By the time early April and the classics rolled around, I was starting to get worried. I had no results and a steady stream of did not finish (DNF) ratings to show for my season. I had managed to finish Het Volk, but that was about it. If I had been on one of the big teams, I would have lost my spot in the selection for sure and would have been relegated to endless training days. But this was a small team, and I was a young rider who still had a lot to learn, so I got to keep my spot. When I received my schedule for the month, it looked like a dream come true:

Three Days of De Panne
Ronde van Vlaanderen (Tour of Flanders)
Gent-Wevelgem
Paris-Roubaix
Amstel Gold Race
Flèche Wallonne
Liège-Bastogne-Liège

I flatted on the first section of cobblestones in the Tour of Flanders. I got a wheel change and was just rolling again when three of my teammates passed me. No one waited. I chased for about 30 km as hard as I could and finally caught the main group when it got stopped by a train. When the tempo lifted again for the hills of the Flemish Ardennes, I found myself in the back of the group. I would never see the front.

After my bleak performances so far, I was looking at Gent-Wevelgem with the same apprehension with which I would have viewed a trip to the dentist. The saving grace was that this was another classic with all its pomp and circumstance, and I loved all of that. I loved rolling up to the sign-in stage and seeing all the reporters and fans and the staging of the pre-race caravan. I didn't even think I would finish the thing, given all of the side-wind stretches. As an amateur, riding through those gusts that pushed you toward the gutter had not been my forte. Actually, it wasn't riding in the side-wind itself but the fact that amateurs could never seem to form more than one echelon.

Gent-Wevelgem takes the riders out of Gent toward the town of Oostende, on the coast, before taking a left turn inland. Every bit of road before Oostende has you staring smack into the wind, which means there isn't much racing going on. After the left turn there's about 60 km of four-lane side-wind and lots of nervous bike racers to contend with.

After we made the turn and the echelons started to form, I found myself toward the tail end of the front echelon on the wheel of Eric Vanderaerden. I was surprised to see how much he was suffering. Vanderaerden was a rider I had read about long before I had even thought about coming to Belgium. In previous years his name had often been spoken in the same breath as that of Eddy

Merckx, but lately he'd been having a hard time living up to his past results.

The tail end of an echelon is a purgatory where your fate is most often changed only by the will of the riders driving the echelon you're in or the ones behind you. We rode flat out. I glanced down at my gears every once in a while to see if there might be a taller one to work with, but of course there never was. Despite that, I was all right and knew I would be able to at least follow Vanderaerden. Keeping toward the front of the race made it possible for me to get over the series of hills—the Rodeberg, the Zwarteberg, and both sides of the Kemmelberg—in reasonable shape. It became clear to me that I might actually be able to race for the finish (as opposed to just trying to find it), despite the fact that I was having a hard time staying at the front. Once the rolling roads that signal the approach to Wevelgem flattened and the big group started to wind up for the sprint, I was able to stand on the pedals just enough to finish alongside some of my heroes. It did not matter to me that my placing was in the fifties or that a group was off the front. I was there for the finish of a classic and started looking forward to Paris-Roubaix.

○ ○ ○

Paris-Roubaix was the first bike race I had ever seen on TV. As I'd watched the mud-soaked riders trying to kill each other while at the same time trying to stay upright on their bikes, I had thought it looked like the hardest race in the world. When I had raced Paris-Roubaix as an amateur, I had entered the Roubaix Velodrome in the second group, sprinting for 7th through 15th places. After 225 km, two flat tires, two crashes, and a broken wheel, I crossed into the velodrome at the front of my group. The problem was that I had never been on a track before and didn't know how to handle the banking. Going into the first turn, I drifted high and was able to regain my composure only after everyone had passed me. I got one place back. On my ride the next day, I went 10 km out of the way just to avoid a 200-meter stretch of small cobblestones.

As we sat in the hotel restaurant the night before my first Paris-Roubaix with the professionals, Roger de Vlaeminck struck up a conversation with Florent. De Vlaeminck was sort of the Steve McQueen of Belgian bike racers. Although most of his generation had gotten bloated and out of shape, De Vlaeminck had stayed fit and still carried himself with the assurance of the star he was. He was then and always will be "Mr. Paris-Roubaix," having won the race four times. I had some personal interest in Roger because my position on the bike was often compared to his.

Shortly into their conversation, he looked over at me and asked Florent, "And what with the American here?"

"*Zijn eerste keer,*" Florent said, sniggering. His first time.

"*Hij zal t' morgen wel weten.*" Tomorrow he'll know. De Vlaeminck smiled at me in such a way that I felt a need to check my pocket to make sure my wallet wasn't missing.

There are a few things in the world that cannot be adequately described with words or pictures. The hell that is Paris-Roubaix is one of them. Standing next to a top fuel dragster or funny car as it launches down the quarter-mile is another. I have done both, so whenever someone I know has the opportunity to see Paris-Roubaix or a professional drag race, I try my best to explain what they will see. No matter how much I gyrate and gesture, no matter how I string together words to describe what they will experience, I always get the same story upon their return: "You wouldn't believe it!" They then proceed to explain it to me, just as inadequately.

The 1988 Paris-Roubaix was the infamous long-breakaway year that saw two lesser-known pros, Dirk Demol and Thomas Wegmüller, sprinting for the win. I was in a small breakaway that got absorbed right at the moment that the winning breakaway left the peloton. It was so early in the race that the team leaders weren't concerned with the group that was going up the road. That was their mistake.

At 10 km out, Werner Wieme, the 28-year-old neopro I was riding in with, and I were told that Demol had just won. It was rough to think that going into the Arenberg forest I had still been with the main group and could have been racing for at least some TV time. Instead, a rookie mistake in leaving the long section of cobblestones there had relegated me to a group that was looking forward to quitting at the second feed zone. The breakaway in front was trying to stay away. The group I had been in at the start of the Wallers section of cobblestones was now racing to catch the leaders, and I, due to my own stupidity, was rolling along with a group of guys who were so happy to be rid of the torture ahead that they were telling jokes. When we rolled up to the last feed zone I expected to climb into the car with the rest of them.

"Come, Joo," Wieme said, and I felt a hand on my back. "You come with me to the finish? It is maybe my only time." I had raced with him a few times with the amateurs.

"*Ja*, OK," I replied and started pedaling again.

He went on to explain that after all of the years he had spent racing with the amateurs, waiting for his chance in the big classics, he would do his best to at least finish those that he started.

With that, he reached into his pocket, grabbed a sawed-off 3-cc syringe, and jabbed the needle through his shorts into his leg.

As an amateur the year before, I had been actually racing at this point, counting down each section of cobblestones and doing my best to win. Now I was just rolling along, not in contention for anything at all. If anything, the marked sections of cobblestones were even more unbearable in this capacity because we were subjected to the jeers of a crowd that had been there for hours. The European fans didn't care that we both wanted to check something off our goals list. To them we were the clown show that existed only to be heckled. It was the only race I ever finished partially covered in beer.

But we did finish. We pedaled all the way to the finish line in front of La Redoute's headquarters in Roubaix. My partner even put his hand on my back before the line, to thank me and let me know that he wanted to be the last rider across the line today. For my efforts, I was officially the youngest rider to finish the race (21) and was awarded a 1,000-French-francs prime (about $165 at the time). I am still waiting to receive that check.

● ● ●

I was cut from our team's start list for Flèche Wallonne. There was part of me that wanted to be on the team but another part that was happy to be able to watch the race on TV instead. I was tired and didn't have the necessary morale to do battle with the Mur de Huy. The Mur, or Wall, is one of the nastiest, steepest stretches of road I have ever seen. It seems to exist only to kick the hell out of bike riders. I have climbed and descended quite a few of the world's great hills, and the thought of the Mur de Huy still causes me pain. Perhaps it was the combination of steepness and length, or perhaps it was my level of fitness on the two occasions that I rode it, but if today you offered me a free trip back to Belgium, I would probably turn you down if it meant I had to climb that hill again. I knew as I watched the race on TV that the couch was the best place for me. I watched Moreno Argentin, Gert-Jan Theunisse, and Steven Rooks climb the Mur de Huy in the big chainring. There are airplanes that climb slower than that.

I had looked forward to the Flemish classics with wide-eyed enthusiasm, but after watching these guys turn the Wall of Huy into a speed bump, I seriously wondered what the hell I was going to accomplish at Liège-Bastogne-Liège. I understood the Flèche Wallonne to be the little brother to Liège, La Doyenne, the grandfather of all classics. I thought L-B-L would surely kill me.

We arrived at a nice hotel, by race hotel standards, and I changed into my requisite Euro tracksuit and assumed the position of a bike racer preparing for the next day's race: flat on my back with my eyes fixed on the little TV. There was nothing worth watching, and by that I mean there was *nothing* worth watching— not like the "Kill Your TV Set" bumper-sticker kind of nothing-on-TV but rather the "I would have killed for a simple *Beverly Hillbillies* or *Alf* rerun, even *Maude* or a soap opera, anything but French and German news" kind of nothing-on-TV. I was out of English-language books by that point, and my magazines were so dog-eared that they were of no further interest to me. My roommate, Cocquyt, was in a similarly foul mood and decided he'd be better off harassing the mechanics. I stayed put. The only real bonus for me at that point was that the weather was generally cool enough during the classics that I could at least sleep pretty well at night. My European teammates never liked to have the window open during the night, so it was not uncommon for me to toss for hours in hotel rooms that were like saunas.

The weather for the 1988 classics season had been easy to deal with so far, and Liège-Bastogne-Liège's weather was more of the same. As a spectator, I would rather see rainy, miserable classic conditions any day, but as a competitor, I was more than happy for another sunny, cold Sunday. I was having a hard time staying motivated to keep myself at the front of the peloton and had contented myself with riding at the very back. In other races, I had noticed that the back was where many of cycling's big names hung out. Of course they all had helpers who would get them out of trouble if a big group split happened and they were left stranded. If my team car could have seen me in the back, I'm sure I would have heard the horn. I might even have gotten a talking-to. But they couldn't see me, so I was safe to zone out for a while, listening to little bits of several conversations and watching the heads of the mass of riders in front of me.

We had turned onto a big road that had a slight downward slope, and I noticed the pace picking up a bit. The wind was now a quartering tailwind from the left. I am not sure if it was just me or if the peloton was becoming more nervous, but I was noticing brakes coming on more frequently, and the *"god verdommes,"* *"putangs,"* and various other curses were becoming more prevalent by the second. I was slowly making my way back to the front when I heard Cocquyt on my left.

"Kom, Joo,*"* he said, *"ze gaat vallen."* Sometimes Cocquyt called me "Joe," but most of the time he pronounced my name the way "Joe" would be read in Flemish, and the tone of his voice, while still reminiscent of the cocky Oost Vlaaming I had come to call

39

a friend, was a little more urgent than usual. He thought "they" were going to crash. I was not sure who "they" were or when or where "they" were going to crash, but I was willing to take his word for it.

Any rider who has ridden in the service of a bigger-name pro has the ability to soft-pedal while riding past another, thereby giving that rider the chance to jump on his wheel and protecting him from any number of different types of wind while making it to the front of the race. Cocquyt was no exception, and the slight pause was all it took for me to check in on the Cocquyt express. We made our way to the absolute front of the giant L-B-L peloton. Patrick was the very first rider in the field, and I was number two. We were moving along at a pretty good pace, right around 50 kph, but the pace was not frantic by any stretch of the imagination, since the wind was primarily from behind us. I had my hands perched on the brake-lever hoods. In this position I would be able to extend my fingers and poke Cocquyt's ass if he moved over on me, or simply bounce off him if I moved over on him too quickly. Since the wind was coming from behind and left, I had my left knuckles prepared for battle. The most dangerous time in a bike race is when the pace drops below a fever pitch but the speed is still high. At the very front, we were safe.

I felt something brush against my right leg and heard the crash. Crashes happen all the time, especially in the classics, where the stakes are so high. Throw in rain, cold, and early-season nerves, and the cocktail is perfect. I didn't risk looking back but instead sneaked a peek under my shoulder. It was the biggest pile of bikes and riders I had ever seen, blocking the four-lane road we were on. Along with Cocquyt and me, Eddy Planckaert and about a dozen others made it through without getting sucked into the crash.

We coasted and soft-pedaled and waited for the survivors to get back to the race. No one would start racing again until every rider was back from the crash. It was an unspoken understanding, and nobody tested it. As the riders from the pile rejoined the group, I was surprised to see how much carnage this *chute* had caused. Sean Kelly had black smudges on his KAS team jersey from sliding along the ground. Other big riders were decorated similarly. I started thinking that this might give me a chance at the end of the day, that these victims would be less motivated and not as strong as they would have been without the crash. The guys started talking about the crash, and I heard different accounts of what had happened. No one worried about *why* it had happened—they only talked about the results. I was surveying the damage on each rider I could see and wasn't paying attention when we started racing again. I was too far back, and on the climb of the Cote de Stokeu I watched the race ride away.

I caught Johan Bruyneel at the bottom of the descent, and the two of us rode together for a while. We both rode in the manner of dropped racers, pushing giant gears around too slowly for any hope of returning to the peloton.

"It's really difficult, the Stokeu, eh?" he said in English, pointing out the obvious.

"*Ja,*" I said. "Steep."

There was a stream of ambulances and helicopters in the area that did not seem to belong in a bike race. Johan answered my question before I could ask it.

"Knickman, his vein is off." He pointed to his neck.

Roy Knickman was a talented American rider whom I had gotten to know a bit that season. I liked him quite a lot. Apart from Bob Roll, Roy was the only guy in the professional peloton I knew

41

well enough to talk to like a regular American. The way Bruyneel described it, I thought Roy was dead for sure. I think there's something about the flow of adrenaline in a heightened situation that affects the way new and disturbing ideas are processed. I began to imagine the whole scenario complete with news reports and a funeral. When you crash, the world slows down. This was the opposite. What little interest I still had in Liège-Bastogne-Liège left the office and went to a funeral.

"I wait for the bus," I told Bruyneel.

Of course, when you want to keep racing, the bus is there behind you like a vulture. When you want the bus to rescue you, it is nowhere to be found. In real time it might have only been minutes before the bus arrived, but to me it felt like hours. I was already off my bike before it came to a stop. I climbed on board.

Roll was already inside. He was sitting about three rows behind the driver, fidgeting with the shoulder of his 7-Eleven jersey. Most of the other losers in the bus looked like they were happy to have been spared the remaining kilometers of road, as I was, but Bob looked angry. Worse yet, Bob looked sort of motivated, even fresh.

"What happened to you?" I asked. "I really didn't expect to see you here." Bob had ridden well the previous year here in the Ardennes.

"Idiots," he said. "These idiots need to learn how to drive. First they try and kill Davis, and then they try and kill me. And they ruined a brand-new jersey!" He fished around in the hole in the jersey for a few seconds.

"And did you hear about Roy?" I asked. "His vein is off," I said, pointing to my neck. I meant to tell Bob that Roy's jugular vein had been severed.

"What happened to Roy?" he asked.

"The helicopters are taking him away. I heard there was blood all over the street," I told him.

Bob went on to explain that the helicopters were not for Knickman but rather for Davis Phinney, a 7-Eleven teammate of Bob's who had crashed through the back of a team car that had stopped on the side of the road. Davis had been accelerating after stopping for another crash and had put his head down for a split second too long. He'd destroyed the back of a parked car, his bike, and his face in the ensuing crash. The rear glass of the car had shattered, and Davis's blood was everywhere.

Bob had also hit a car, and when the race was over I got to see the damage. The car's custom welded-steel rack, designed to carry at least four bikes and a ton of wheels, was destroyed. The impact from Bob flying into the rack had not only mangled many of the spare wheels arrayed across the trunk but killed at least one of the bikes and rendered the rack unusable. The back of the car and its roof were wounded too from the roughly two hundred pounds of dude and bike that had assaulted it at 56 kph. I had to laugh, imagining the poor guys inside the car as a 7-Eleven bomb from Northern California hit it.

3

Kermis Don't Play Fair

WITH THE CLASSICS NOW OVER, THE MEAT-AND-POTATOES WORK
of a small Belgian team could begin: kermis racing. Despite popular opinion, racing a kermis was not all about the drugs. Most
riders who have not immersed themselves in Belgian bike racing,
or who haven't given themselves enough time to understand the
inner workings of this type of race, will speak of a kermis as some
sort of drug-crazed freak-fest. And it's true that kermis races can
be scary places for the uninitiated because many of the rules that
apply to all other forms of bike racing don't apply to the kermis.
If the grand tours are like classical music, kermis racing is punk
rock, Belgian-style.

"Kermis" is Flemish for "carnival" and comes complete with
rides and games and lots of salty, fried food. If you have read anything at all about cycling in Belgium, you have undoubtedly come
across the word *"kermesse,"* which is the French term for these

events. But calling them by the French name is blasphemous in Flemish-speaking Belgium, where most of these races are found. Cycling in Belgium is more Flemish than French. Since you need slightly warmer temperatures for people to enjoy a carnival, there are only classics and semiclassics until May, and then the kermis races begin.

They're all about the same length, 150–180 km, with a circuit length of not less than 10 km (the amateur races are shorter). I didn't understand the significance of the course length until I dropped out of one and watched the rest of it from a café. I found myself as interested in the people watching the race as the race itself. The time it takes for the pros to cover 10 km is almost exactly the time it takes to order, receive, and drink a beer. A lead car announces the arrival of the first riders with some terrible accordion music, which acts as a signal that it's time to drain that last bit from the glass and get outside.

There was almost always one pro kermis per day from June through September, so the tension you'd witness at the start line of a classic was completely absent. Instead you'd see the riders joking with each other. If there were 125 riders entered, 50 of them probably did not even intend to finish the race. They may have been ordered to start by their teams, or they may just have wanted some fast training for an hour or so. Of the remaining group, there would be specialist kermis riders and kermis teams who headlined the sports pages, racking up win after win against seemingly superior competition. Sprinkled in were young riders hoping to catch the eye of their director and get a spot on the squad for a big race. There were also a few cycling superstars getting some race training, whether they lived in Belgium or were just passing through.

Since the majority of the racers didn't consider these races important, there was seldom any rhyme or reason to the flow of the events. For instance, at some point during the 1988 kermis season, our team was invited to a small stage race in France, but Florent had made an agreement for us to race a big kermis close to Brugge. By "big," I mean only that it was a kermis with a long history. The problem was that in order to make it to the stage race for its start, we would have to leave Belgium less than an hour into the race. Cocquyt decided that we should go as hard as we possibly could from the gun, team time trial style, and then peel off at the end of the 11-km lap, laughing at all the guys we had tortured. Of course, we all coughed up blood for the entire trip into France, but it was strangely worth it, as if we had smashed our guitars, poured beer on the audience, and walked offstage before the end of the first song. Punk rock.

I saw my first pro kermis as a spectator during my first week in Belgium, and it felt like trying to escape a hall of mirrors but not being able to read the exit signs. Everything was larger than life and more grotesque than I had imagined. In places, the kermis air reeks of *fritjes*, salt-cured fish, fried sausages, and Belgian-style hamburgers. Though the sights and smells probably conjure up beautiful, innocent memories for many people, it was a great gauntlet of stench for me when I began racing kermises and had to suck their air deep into my lungs.

When I had called Jim Ochowicz to tell him I was going to keep my job with Florent, he had warned against it, saying that kermis racers were a dime a dozen and that a real bike racer needs to aspire to big races. I agreed with him, but I explained that while I was surely going to be expected to do some kermis races, I was also guaranteed the chance to race the classics and many of the

47

smaller stage races. This, of course, was as much an explanation to me as it was to him; I was trying to sell myself on the idea. How many chances does one get to ride with the most important American cycling team? And how many of these stupid kermis races would I be able to handle?

This was only my second calendar year as a pro, and I was not willing to admit that my future had limits. The way to superstardom in rock and roll is most always a few years spent in smoky bars and living in a passenger van, but the way to superstardom on the bicycle is almost never reached after too much time on the kermis circuit. Kermis races will make you tough and fast very quickly, but they will also make you incapable of climbing anything longer than a freeway overpass in about the same amount of time. The races I had done the previous year had all been thrilling to me whether they were classics, small stage races, or even the lowliest of kermis races. Unfortunately, I was now in that dangerous realm of thinking I was smarter and better than I actually was. In other words, as a cyclist I was not yet wise enough to know how much I still needed to learn. Although the big races will abuse you straight to your face, the kermis race won't play fair at all. I was a blind man trying to win a shell game.

The sheer adrenaline of the previous year had let me gut it out to the finish of the races I'd entered, but these first kermis races didn't go so well. I found myself missing giant splits and quitting races before the halfway point. Sometimes I quit when I didn't really want to; when everyone else in your forty-man group turns right after crossing the finish line halfway through the race and heads for the showers, it's tough to soldier on alone. You could justify quitting a race on the kermis circuit because there was always another race. Miss the split today? Try again tomorrow.

"Morgen is een andere dag." Tomorrow is another day. But with the string of DNFs and also-rans that I was piling up, the consolation from the old Belgian fans was starting to feel more like heckling than support.

At about the time all hope was lost, I fell solidly, squarely, ass-backward into greatness, finding myself in the deciding breakaway of a kermis race. It was the perfect mix of riders and teams, so we quickly gained a lead of 1.5 minutes, and the team cars were allowed to join us. I think I was waiting for some congratulatory gesture from the Eurotop team car, but it was just another day at the office for these guys, and they only wanted to see that I was okay. I think they also wanted to make sure that it was, in fact, me, Joe, in the breakaway.

This was the time before radio communication between riders and team directors, and the race behind the race, the race among the directors in their team cars, was in many cases as important as anything that was going on with the riders. Surely there have been many improvements in cycling over the years, but radio communication is not one of them. Radios have pushed up speeds and made racing more dangerous because, with the directors shouting instructions nonstop, everyone is keyed up and nervous all the time. The time of team cars and the games the directors played inside them was always interesting, and Florent was one of the masters of the follow caravan. He could bring himself up to me and drop back with such ease that you'd think George Balanchine had choreographed the whole thing. Part of the importance of the team car at this point was to assure me that I was really in the breakaway and that I would have to pay attention.

As it became clear that I would be finishing in the top group for the first time that year, I had to weigh the situation. There were

49

nine riders in the breakaway, which meant that at worst I would take home ninth place. To a guy with nothing to show for his season, a top 10 was just fine. I continued to take my turns at the front of the group, hoping we would stay away until the finish.

I was so happy to be in the front, racing a bike race again, that I did not catch the fact that a deal for the win was being made. Everyone was part of the deal but me. The breakaway rode together like a decent team time trial squad with everyone taking his turn, which was not surprising because everyone else had a common goal: 7,000 francs. Seven thousand francs was roughly equivalent to $200 at the time, which even now doesn't seem like enough money to sell a race for, but it was pretty much the going rate. You'd never think of selling a race for that amount if you were with a smaller group, but in a group this large the overall cost was going to be more than a thousand bucks. I would probably have continued on, oblivious to the deal, if my team car had not come back up to talk to me.

"Are you in the deal?" Albert asked me in Flemish.

"*Nee,*" I responded. "There's a deal?"

"Of course there is, dummy. Why do you think they are all so content with each other? You must attack. When they take you back, you must go again and again, until they speak with you. Understand?"

I nodded and joined the rotation. I rode through a couple of times and then dropped off the back, about a bike length, so they would think I was waiting for the team car again. As two or three riders came to the back and looked at me to jump in, I barked the short, staccato *"Ja"* that told them to grab the wheel coming through because I was staying out of the rotation for a minute. And then I went, swinging to the opposite side of the road, standing up and sprinting like it was the last kilometer of the race. I counted about thirty pedal revolutions and then peeked under my arm. They were closing quickly. Just before they caught me, I sat up and slowed. If there had been no deal in place, there would have been a counterattack right away, but this breakaway kept rolling along. I drifted just off the back and went again. This time they were a little quicker with the chase, so I went again just before they caught me, swinging to the opposite side of the road again. Again I was chased down. I let myself rest for just one rotation before attacking the group for the last time.

"God verdomme!" I heard as I jumped in front of the group. Of course I knew I was not going anywhere, but whoever was supposed to win that race was going to have to do something quickly about me or the rest of the riders would start to follow my lead. Sure enough, as soon as I got caught, I was presented with an offer.

"Seven toussands," he said in English.

"Zeven duizand?" I asked, pronouncing it "sayin doosht," as it would be pronounced in my region's dialect. This was more of a weak tactic than a polite gesture. Although many of the riders knew I could understand a bit of the language, most of them thought they could sneak through some slang or some strong dialect and I would be lost. I might have been a little naive when it came to race deals, but I wanted them to know they'd have to really whisper to keep me out of the loop.

When the team car came back, Albert asked if everything was okay. I mouthed the word "seven" to him. He shot me a knowing smile, and I went back to work. The rest was easy. We continued to ride hard and successfully stayed away from the main peloton. With about 2 km to go, the Isoglass team rider, who now owned the race, attacked and nobody chased. Having spent much of my life in the American South, I expected the rest of us would make a show of it, as they did for pro wrestling in Memphis, but there was nothing. This guy had just paid roughly a grand for a race that even his mother didn't care about, and the rest of us didn't even light the candles on his cake. At 1 km to go, when there was a sufficient gap between the winner and us, we started racing again. I managed to not be the last guy in the group. Johan Museeuw was second, nearly catching our benefactor.

Over the years I have recounted the stories of selling kermis races, and the response has run from shocked disbelief and anger to fascination. My experience as a pro cyclist in Europe has left me with a somewhat altered moral code, such that many of the things that bother normal people are invisible to me. This race that I sold would not be the last. In fact, I was able to make good spending money by making it into the breakaway and then attacking at precisely the right moment if I thought a deal was forming. A rider from the town where the race is being held will often want to win more than anything else in the world. Think of this as Homecoming for bike racers. As such, the local café might offer him a small bonus for winning in front of his people. Most likely, he would also receive a bonus from his team. Add to that the prize money, assuming he didn't have to split it with any teammates, and his cost for buying a kermis race could be reasonable. I liked selling races to sprinters because they were only asking for me to ride hard in the breakaway. They always made my dilemma easier, too, by buying enough other help that sneaking away in the last few kilometers was impossible. In the end, I would sprint as hard as I could but still get beaten like I was driving a lawn tractor in a car race.

As an amateur I found that kermis races with fewer riders were easier to race, with the deciding breakaway coming early. In the pro ranks it was different. In the pros, smaller fields meant not only fewer riders but also fewer good riders. Many of the specialist kermis riders liked amphetamines, which changed the rider's performance in a number of different ways. The most interesting of these to watch was the feeling of euphoria and loss of inhibition. It made these guys want to attack again and again. They weren't necessarily able to go any faster, but they were always ready to go. The races would start and stop, going from zero to sixty back to zero many times per lap. Many of these riders became so blinded by self-confidence that they'd even become combative when I tried to go with them in an attack. One of the telltale signs that my competitors were "good" was when they would suddenly speak to me in English. As I started finding my way into more and more breakaways, the other riders found out that I could understand everything they were saying. Because of this, they really had no need to speak in English, but when these guys were jacked on amphetamines, it was often like they were my new best buddies. Frequently they giggled like little kids at a slumber party, speaking English the whole time.

I went through phases when it came to this uniquely Belgian race. There were many ups and downs for me during my career; most of them were due to my own fitness or lack of it. The interesting thing about the kermis races, though, is that my love or hate of them came less from my fitness than from the riders in the race. If I had to do more than one of the smaller races in a row, I would start complaining. On the other hand, I truly loved the big kermises where whole teams would show up and the head sport director would drive the car. With the bosses in the car, the team couldn't just screw around for a while and let a group of guys get up the road so that they could go home. With the bosses present, you'd often see the big teams chasing down breakaways because they had all been hanging out at the back talking about their cars. Of course, these dudes were chasing grudgingly after what they considered to be inferior competition and often failed miserably. I loved that. I loved seeing the big teams fall flat on their faces. The teams that were hopped up on designer drugs a couple of months before would harp about the kermis teams being drug-addled wastes of space while they were chasing in vain on only three cylinders. Call it a classic case of the pot calling the kettle black; in this case I was more inclined to side with the kettle. I did not view the big teams as the eight-hundred-pound gorilla, but I am always curious when the guy who brings a machine gun to a fistfight cries "foul."

● ● ●

Even though my team didn't concentrate heavily on kermis races, we were expected to perform whenever we entered as a team. Florent, like most of the directors of that time, was from the generation of cycling that bred great riders such as Eddy Merckx, Freddy Maertens, and Roger de Vlaeminck, and the mentality was that every race was important. While they wouldn't specially prepare for smaller races, when the gun went off, riders like these treated every race like their last. The problem with my team was that it sucked. We had some neopros who lacked any discernible talent. We had some Dutch riders who seemed to be more interested in shooting amphetamines than any sort of racing. We had some second- and third-year pros who would never get another contract. Some of these guys never understood how a team works in a bike race. And then there were Cocquyt and me.

Cocquyt and I started riding well together in the kermis races, often finding ourselves in the same breakaway. If there was money being handed out, we didn't hesitate to hold out our hands.

By July I couldn't stand to be around most of the team. Cocquyt and I would find our own place to get dressed, away from the rest of the guys. When this wasn't possible and I was forced to interact with my teammates, I was amazed at what I saw. Imagine your favorite sitcom, throw in four or five different dialects, shave fifty points off everyone's IQ so that all conversation is reduced to the basic essentials of life (cars, food, sex, and performance-enhancing drugs), and then add some intravenous and/or subcutaneous drug use and you'll have a good picture of the kermis race dressing room. Of course all of the characters in this sitcom were males except when one of the teammates brought his wife or girlfriend in so she could wash him.

The more senior riders in the squad were handing out drugs like candy to the younger guys. If the young guys had been better riders, this might have been even more deplorable, but these were riders who would only get another contract if there were suddenly a rider shortage. Since they couldn't really help the team, their only redeeming quality was their amusement value. Watching these amped-up idiots bounce off their own selves for part of the race was much-needed comic relief and my compensation for being forced to get dressed with them.

The two riders I had the least amount of patience for were Leon Nevels and Leo Boelhouwers. Nevels had turned pro in 1983 and, despite what seemed to be a reasonable amount of natural talent, had resigned himself to jabbing his arms with needles several times before each race. There is a line crossed when a rider is no longer injecting amphetamines so that he can race but racing so that he can inject amphetamines. Nevels couldn't even see that line anymore. He rode every criterium he could get a contract for and every kermis that didn't conflict with a criterium. To hear him speak of it, he was jacked up for every race.

His drug of choice came in a 10-cc *potje* that was brewed up in some Dutch equivalent of a trailer-park meth lab. He was going through a lot of the stuff because every time I saw him he had a new *potje*, and each was always sure to be better than the last. He had a fascination with how well the clear liquid flowed down the glass after he swirled it around, and he wanted us all to see it. The more smoothly the liquid flowed down the glass inside the *potje*, the better the drug, I guessed. At one race, he was so insistent that we all see how "pure" this new *potje* was that I was forced to swirl the thing around a bit and then examine the flow.

"Dude, there's a hair in here," I said. Cocquyt snatched the *potje* and took a look.

"Nevels, you stupid chicken, it looks like a dog hair too," he laughed. "Maybe you should ask that dog for your money back."

Nevels was a dope fiend, but he was largely harmless. Boelhouwers, on the other hand, could cause real trouble for anyone unlucky enough to be riding nearby. He was in his second year as a pro, having ridden for Florent's team the year before. He was from the Dutch province of Limburg and was hard to understand. Even native speakers had a difficult time understanding him, as what came out of his mouth was a combination of the dialect of Limburg and his own feral speech pattern. Boelhouwers was constantly looking for drugs from the other guys on the team and would take anything anyone gave him, from a cough drop to a nitroglycerine tablet to a dip from one of Nevels's *potjes*.

In the context of sports, most people equate amphetamines with an increased level of performance, but this is not always the case. Although amphetamines do have a tendency to make good bike racers better, they only made Boelhouwers more of an idiot. He would attack at the wrong time and from the wrong place. He would wait for a teammate to attack and then chase him down. He would wobble around, bouncing off everyone, and spout gibberish. And in almost all of these cases he was laughing. On more than one occasion Boelhouwers took so much of something before and perhaps during the race that he puked all over our dressing room floor after the race was over.

Cocquyt was more tolerant of Boelhouwers than I. In fact, I think he even liked having a half-witted jester on the team, since he could get Boelhouwers to do tricks like a beer-drinking circus monkey. What Cocquyt did have a problem with was the Limburger's constant drug mooching. To Cocquyt, this was equivalent to that friend who eats your food and always drinks your last beer but never has anything for you when the shoe's on the other foot. For weeks he gave Boelhouwers a hard time, ribbing him every time he asked somebody for something. But then one day Cocquyt relented and handed him a small green pill.

"Goed voor de lucht," Cocquyt announced, making a gesture to show his lungs opening up. Good for the air.

Boelhouwers didn't hesitate; he didn't even look at the pill. He just tossed it into his mouth and swallowed. I was surprised by what I had just witnessed. Cocquyt was not really Mr. Generosity, and he had just given something to the biggest knucklehead on the team. I was able to get his attention, and he winked.

"Ansiolin," he mumbled. *"Goed voor de lucht."* Patrick was pretty cool, but I knew that even he had to be holding back a laugh. Ansiolin is an Italian brand name for diazepam. In the United States, the most common brand name for it is Valium. He had just given a serious tranquilizer to a guy getting ready to do a bike race. One pill was 6 milligrams, a dosage that probably wouldn't knock Boelhouwers out but would certainly render him sleepier than anything that truly was *"goed voor de lucht."*

The race we were preparing for was one of the fastest kermis races of the year, with wide roads and only one true corner. I used the 53x14 on the rollout and after that only needed the bottom two gears. "Fun" is not a word I would typically use to describe a kermis race, but this race was fun. The giant peloton and huge roads made it so that you could race if you wanted or sit in and enjoy the scenery at 60 kph. I was feeling okay and stayed up at the front after the first couple of laps. I made it into the big split at the tail end of the race, but despite jumping with every attempt to get away, I sprinted for the bottom half of the prize money.

Fast races like this one were energizing as well as satisfying, and rolling back to the café where we had gotten dressed with Cocquyt and another teammate, Theo Muis, I felt like I had at least another hundred kilometers in my legs, which felt great. Boelhouwers was already there, slouching in his chair, still in his race clothing and with a more-confused-than-usual look on his face. His clothing was messed up more than it would have been from just the race. It seems that the combination of sedative drugs combined with his already diminished brain function had altered his judgment as well as his bike-handling skills. After missing the split, he'd somehow misjudged the distance between himself and a car parked on the side of the road. After bouncing off the car, he'd careened off the road and crashed into a ditch. Incredibly, Boelhouwers asked Cocquyt if he could have some more of that pill that was *"goed voor de lucht."*

○ ○ ○

Since Belgium is such a flat country, most kermis races on the calendar lack any natural separators like hills, so they often split up more from luck than from rider talent. This is not to say that the races aren't hard—they're actually brutal beasts with the ability to steal a rider's morale in the blink of an eye. A good result in a kermis race was discounted because it was just a kermis. A bad result in a kermis race promised ridicule and a tongue-lashing from any number of people.

Oostende is a thirteenth-century town located on the North Sea. It is a favorite seaside getaway spot for many Belgians and the location of my favorite kermis race. The wind that whips through the downtown section of the course is nearly strong enough to knock the riders off their bikes, but once the race gets out into the open fields, just outside town, that same wind rips the peloton apart. Echelons form immediately, and the side-wind battle that is so specific to races in Belgium and Holland begins.

Side-wind was to me as the mountains are for a climber; I was always excited when the peloton decimated itself at the start of one of these sections of wind. I had a hint that I might be good in the side-wind when I found myself in the front echelon in Gent-Wevelgem early in the year. That notion was reinforced when Jelle Nijdam punched me on the side of my butt for jumping ahead of him in the rotation at a semiclassic in Holland. Here, as at the bigger races, the peloton would regroup after the sections of side-wind, but the size of that group would become smaller and more manageable after each lap. This kind of racing starts wearing at you the longer you hang on, and I began to feel like I was bowling a perfect game in which each new frame was becoming more pressure-filled. I'd have to say that I bobbled on the last lap, leaving a few pins standing. Still, I was happy with the result.

○ ○ ○

In his 1990 book, *Rough Ride,* Paul Kimmage revealed many of the evils of professional cycling, most notably doping. He talked about the pressures he faced to take drugs as a cyclist and the careers and lives derailed by doping. I was given a copy immediately after the book was released and read it cover to cover. Kimmage told a story of trying to race the kermis in Oostende. He painted a picture of the pain and suffering this race inflicted, and stopped just short of implying that everyone in the race, except him, was loaded to the gills on amphetamines.

I met Paul in 1988 during the Midi Libre stage race in southern France. Perhaps it is different for a person coming from Ireland to live and race in Europe, but for me, as an American, having the chance to speak English with someone who had English as his native tongue was a great bonus, and I took every opportunity to try to talk with Paul. Most of the other English speakers I'd raced with were happy to have a conversation where we didn't have to restructure our sentences. But Paul wasn't interested; it seemed as if he was annoyed by my attempts to talk with him. If he had been a top-level pro like Sean Kelly or Stephen Roche, I might have been less confused by the cold reception, but Paul was just another rider who hadn't won anything, kind of like me.

On the day we met, we were both in the bus, the big group of riders at the tail end of the race who are unable to follow the climbers in the hills. Once you get relegated to the bus, your hard day is over and you continue on, milking the clock. Your only job is to make it to the finish before the time cutoff. Often the official language of these groups is Flemish/Dutch with bits of the other cycling languages thrown in. Flemish/Dutch is the official language because flatlanders are often in trouble once the race makes its way into the mountains.

To give him the benefit of the doubt, I'd guess that Kimmage must have already given up on his career as a cyclist at this point because his tone during the short conversation we had was tired, bitter, and cynical, like the tone of his book. He made excuses for being in this group; he didn't feel that it was at all his own fault he'd ended up with the losers and thought that if he had not been forced to work for his team leader he would surely have been with the leaders. As sour as it was, I enjoyed the short conversation, although I didn't bother coming back for seconds.

At the Oostende race, Paul was moving around in the peloton during the first couple of laps. As with any new discipline, it takes a race or two to figure out kermis racing. Paul, like any other newcomer, did not flow with the race. Even though professional cycling is an international sport, there were types of racing that normal riders like me and Kimmage and the majority of the professional peloton needed to first figure out before we could hope to be competitive. Paul could have taken every performance-enhancing drug available at the time, but I doubt it would have made any real difference for him at Oostende. My own preparation for the race in Oostende was the same as it was for almost every kermis race: three delicious tarts from a local bakery, half a Coke, some lukewarm tea in the bottle, and a couple of Animine (caffeine) tablets in the pockets just in case.

4

Rolling with Eurotop

I WAS EXCITED TO HEAR THAT WE HAD BEEN INVITED TO THE Grand Prix Midi Libre in the south of France. The Midi Libre, which died in 2002 from lack of funds, was in its time considered good preparation for the Tour de France because it covered many of the same Pyrenean roads used in July's great race. I was happy to be able to get out of Belgium for a while and get back to the mountains.

In true small-team fashion, we were to pile as many people we could into as few vehicles as possible and head off to the Midi. I had taken delivery of our team's third car, a Citroën limousine that was a hand-me-down from the former ANC Halfords team from Britain. It lacked the red-white-and-black Eurotop livery of our other three vehicles, which could have been a problem had I been caught speeding in it. Driving a car sporting official Euro-top colors (or any other team colors, for that matter) was roughly equivalent to driving with a diplomatic license plate. We got away with a lot more than the average civilian—speeding, passing on the shoulder, bump-drafting, even splitting lanes were all acceptable when driving a team car.

The standard operating procedure for Belgian teams traveling into France was for everyone to assemble in Kortrijk, just inside the border on the Belgium side, and proceed from there. The mechanics would collect each rider's bike, and then we would head out, the cars in one caravan and the mechanics on their own, since they would be driving a slower truck and be subject to more intense scrutiny at the border crossings.

We planned our rendezvous for 8 A.M. I typically awoke at 5:30 or 6, so picking up Cocquyt and heading off to the meeting place did not even require me to set my alarm. As long as I was at his house by 7:15 or so, we'd be on time. At 7:30 the phone rang, and Albert's daughter Els woke me up. It was Cocquyt, wondering where I was. Shit. Of all the times to sleep in, I picked this one! Less than ten minutes later I was driving the big Citroën at 180 kph along the same canal road Cocquyt and I used for training. The speed limit was 90 kph. I was having fun. After living the life of a monk for the past several months, making the big, pillowy French car wallow through the gradual turns on the narrow canal road was just what the doctor ordered. I completely forgot the fact that the rest of the team and Florent were going to be pissed. When we showed up at the hotel parking lot, the team van and mechanics were already gone. Nobody said anything about the fact that we were forty-five minutes late. We left Cocquyt's bike in the trunk of the Citroën and headed south.

I generally disliked driving anywhere with the team. Belgians hate having any sort of a draft flow over their bodies. They also hate air conditioning. By the time I had graduated from high school, my family had moved eight times. By the time I came to

Belgium, I had lived in six different states. I spent all of my formative years in climates that are warm, if not hot, and in some cases extremely humid. For me, indoor temperatures should be cool and comfortable; outdoor should be warm or hot. In the team car, sweat would be running down our faces, but no one in the car would allow a window to be cracked or a vent to pass the slightest hint of outside air. Most of the cars we drove didn't even have air conditioning, and the big Citroën was no different. But I had volunteered to take the first driving stint, and since Cocquyt was my only passenger, I switched on the vents and aimed the air at my face. It wasn't air conditioning, but it was enough.

We were on the Périphérique, the ring road around Paris, roughly three hours from where we'd started, when boredom set in.

"Maybe you should test the ABS," Cocquyt urged in a tone reminiscent of everything I'd ever heard as a kid just before I did something that got me into trouble.

Antilock braking systems in cars were still rare in 1988, and it was fun to check out the new technology. We were doing 140 kph when I mashed the brake pedal to the floor. We were in the right lane, and the wall that was just a few feet away from the passenger's side of the car started getting closer. Although 75 percent of the ABS system was doing its job, one of the wheels had locked up, upsetting the balance of an already boatlike car and sending us toward the wall. Anyone who has ever raced any kind of vehicle knows that crashing is simply the unfortunate by-product of trying. Even so, I wasn't going to be able to make any money racing Citroën limousines, so hitting the wall wasn't a necessary part of my education. I lifted the brake pedal; we straightened out and kept going.

"Piece-of-shit auto," Cocquyt pointed out, in English. I agreed.

● ● ●

Time trials in 1988 were still ridden without aero bars, meaning that the rider's natural position on the bike was a key part of his success as a time trialist. Luckily, I was gifted with a natural aerodynamic position; on the "Delta" bikes of the day, with their small front wheels and cow-horn handlebars, I could almost always find myself in the top 10 or 15 places in any time trial under 30 km.

After a pre-race lap of the prologue time trial course for the Midi Libre, I was confident that I would be able to get myself a podium spot. It was a perfect course for me, shortish and very fast, with a downhill start and an uphill finish. For most time trials, I preferred to reconnoiter the course with a couple of easy laps to take in the proper lines and find potential obstacles. I would call my mission good after just this surface glimpse and then get back to whatever pre-race preparation I had time for, which most likely consisted of donning earphones to blast Metallica straight into my frontal lobe. The Midi's prologue course was just too much fun, though, and I tested my lines through the turns several times, each at high speed. I figured I would need a bigger gear since I always felt better fighting the bike than spinning high revs on this sort of a course. I was even able to talk the mechanics into giving me a 55-tooth front chainring, replacing the 53 I'd had on the bike.

Prologue time trials are strange events. For the most part, they are simply a photo-op for professional and amateur photographers and a chance for the fans to see each rider as he passes by on the course. They seldom affect the outcome of the race. There are few riders who take the start of a stage race with even the most distant notion that they might win the prologue. Yet few riders sandbag the prologue. It is not uncommon for a rider who has placed in the teens or twenties in the prologue to find himself in the leader's jersey after a long breakaway on the first stage. Imagine the horror of finding yourself in a breakaway with a huge lead, only to learn at the end of the day that you would be second in the overall classification because you had not given it your all in the prologue. Whole careers have been launched based upon a leader's jersey in just one small stage race. Given that fact, riders spend most of the prologue day fretting about the race and warming up for it. Afterward, many riders, including me, will find themselves coughing up what feels like portions of lung for most of the night.

When my time came to launch, I was completely ready. I had warmed up sufficiently and gotten to the start podium on time but not too early. I was excited but not too nervous. I was a poster child for 1950s-style, buttoned-down preparedness. When the clock ticked through 30 seconds to go, I began to breathe a little more deeply, hoping my lungs might not take a terrible beating during the first seconds of the race. I backpedaled a couple of revolutions and then positioned my legs and feet so I could get off the podium as fast as possible. The clock ticked through 10 seconds to go, and I focused on the second hand. At 5 seconds to go the clock began its *beep, beep, beep, beep, beep,* and then the higher-pitched *beep* to start my race.

What follows is almost always the most anticlimactic second of bike racing. The noise of the clock, the launch ramp, the pomp and circumstance of the time trial start—it all comes together to make riders and spectators alike expect some sort of explosion, like a rocket launch. In reality, it is more of a gasp for air and a slow roll down a short ramp followed by a thud as the wheels make contact with the road. In my case, there was almost always a slight pause as I collected myself after my arms nearly collapsed when the overinflated front tire hit the pavement.

The Midi's prologue start was different, though, as the ramp was pointing downhill. I was able to get on top of the gear so quickly that I could enjoy the loud clunking sound from the rear disk wheel caused by shifting into higher gears. I hit the first turn fast enough to coast through it for fear of clipping a pedal on the ground. The next stretch curved gradually through the trees and leveled off a bit. I had no problem staying on top of the huge gear. I never bobbled at all in that section and prepared for the next turn. I grabbed an easier gear and pedaled through it. Again there were no bobbles, no mistakes, and I stared ahead toward the final right-hander. I stood up, 30 meters or so before the turn, so I could keep up my momentum. I was able to see the finish line. All I needed was a couple hundred meters of suffering. With about 75 meters to go, I sat down and reached for the shift lever. I needed one more tooth. Then I stood back up and fought the bike across the line.

I couldn't hear my time being broadcast over the loudspeakers, but I was sure I had nailed it. I soft-pedaled to the team car to grab my jacket and legwarmers.

"Third," barked my teammate Pascal van der Vorst.

"Shit!" How was that possible? I racked my brain to find the reason why I did not own the number-one spot. Was it the gear selection going into the finish straightaway? Had I needed a bigger gear in the start? Had I needed a smaller gear in the start? Still,

I was convinced that I would be in the top five at the end of the day. There were only twenty-some riders left to go, and the odds were against many of them sneaking in under my time. I knew I had gone pretty much as fast as anyone could go over that course on a bike.

When the results sheets came out, I scanned the top five for my name, but it wasn't there. I moved down a few more spots, but I still wasn't listed. I kept going. I went back to the top. Surely there had been a mistake. I had worked through the top 15 or so several times now, and there was no mention of Joseph Parkin. I turned to the back page, thinking I might have been relegated or disqualified somehow, but my name wasn't listed there either. I flipped back to the front page again. I carefully worked through each place until I found my name standing prominently toward the top of page 2. Twenty-three riders had ridden the short prologue course faster than I had. "Wrong answer" buzzers from terrible TV game shows sounded in my brain, and my size 38 chest deflated a bit. I had ripped off what I'd thought was a pole-position lap but instead had been handed a severe beating. People say that as long as you go with your A game and give it your best, you can be proud no matter what the outcome. I am sure that is true some of the time—I may even have said it myself on occasion—but sponsors are not interested in the journey; they are interested in the outcome. If that was the best I could do with a race and a course that suited me, where nothing went wrong, what was I going to give the sponsors? I had a hard time sleeping that night.

Many Belgian riders were using the Midi Libre as an *"ontweningskuur"* or detox period. At home in Belgium, they felt the pressure to perform in every race and so they would chemically prepare themselves with all kinds of products prominently listed on the antidoping list. But the national championships were coming up, and the idea was that if you raced clean during the mountainous, weeklong stage race, you could come back to Belgium, add some jet fuel, and do well at the championship. As such, the mood in the Belgian camp was casual and calm. As soon as the road went up, great laughing groups of nonclimbing Belgians formed to make sure everybody got to the finish within the allotted time. Mortal enemies just a few hundred kilometers north were now best buddies, laughing at the expense of anyone who unwittingly offered himself up be sacrificed.

On day two, we were rolling through a long, winding canyon late in the day's stage. The temperature was a little too hot for most of the Belgians, and many of them were out of water. My teammate Pascal van der Vorst offered some of his bottle to fellow Belg and former Tour de France green-jersey winner Frank Hoste. The big sprinter from Gent was parched and ever so thankfully sucked the contents from the bottle. Van der Vorst was a tall, goofy-looking strawberry blond with huge hair and a disproportionately skinny lower body. His legs and butt were so skinny that he had to wear size small or extra-small shorts even though he was six-foot-two and 165 pounds or so, and even those didn't hug his legs very tightly. Although his legs and butt were birdlike, certain other lower body parts could better be described as horselike, and Van der Vorst scared old ladies and school children like a circus freak. A couple of Hoste's ADR teammates had seen the exchange between the former green-jersey winner and the freak. Within minutes every Flemish-speaking bike racer, team director, mechanic, soigneur, and journalist in France knew what was happening and was part of a conspiracy to make Hoste think that Van der Vorst had some sort of *ehh-pah-tee-teece* and that, by drinking from the bottle, he was most likely going to have hepatitis too.

After the race, as Hoste consulted with the team's soigneur and director, José de Cauwer, his teammates were already busy bringing the conspiracy back to Belgium by contacting his wife and family doctor. Played on anyone else, this probably would have been the cruelest of practical jokes, but Frank was as gullible and innocent as a kindergartener that wants a puppy—just too ripe for the picking. Various experts in reversing the effects of water bottle—transmitted hepatitis, including another green-jersey winner and Hoste's ADR roommate, Eddy Planckaert, were consulted.

The initial treatment was garlic. Hoste was told to eat raw garlic, entire bulbs of the stuff. In a show of empathy, Planckaert joined Hoste in the treatment. After dinner Hoste, normally a nondrinker, was instructed to down three or four shots of cognac. After this he was to get into a bathtub full of ice for ten minutes and then quickly get into his hotel bed, the sheets of which were now covered in peeled garlic cloves. If this treatment did not work, Hoste was going to have to fly back to Belgium for blood transfusions and a possible liver replacement. By the next day the joke had spread to other languages—French, Italian, and Spanish. Hoste was sure that he was screwed. The two ADR teammates transformed the smell of the Midi region into a great, rolling garlic farm, something that reminded me of driving through Gilroy, California. Late in the day somebody let the poor guy off the hook, and by the end of the stage race the garlic had left his body.

● ● ●

The Midi Libre progressed as most small stage races did for me. I would have one good day followed by one not-so-good day. One day I would be with the French, Italian, and Spanish speakers at the front of the race, going uphill in the mountains, and the next day I would be holding on to the tail end of the laughing group, speaking Flemish.

After the initial disappointment with my prologue result, I was coming around and having some fun. I loved the Pyrenean descents. I loved seeing how fast I could pass an entire peloton after dropping to the back of the follow caravan to pick up Cokes and water bottles. For a time I believed I was one of the fastest riders in the world on mountain descents. Television fans of the Grand Tours have long been led to believe that the guys who go over the hills up front are the great downhill riders, but that is not entirely true. With few exceptions, the fastest riders downhill are some of the slower riders going up the other side. It may be a survival technique or simply a reward for the suffering imposed by the climbers, but there are few things better in the world than descending narrow mountain roads at 90-plus kph.

As an added attraction, I liked to take the inside line in turns on the team cars and get as close to the front door as possible. Most of the directors had these roads memorized, but some had their hands full just getting the car to the bottom. The looks on their faces as I passed inches from their mirrors was priceless.

At the bottom of the descent of the Col du Jau, I had successfully passed most of the peloton and was comfortably riding in the top five or ten spots when we suddenly ran out of descent and the road pitched up steeply. Only a few minutes earlier, I had studied the course graphic card I had in my pocket, and I knew a climb was coming, but this wall staring at me was a surprise, both physically and emotionally. The Belgians liken what happened to me on this short climb to putting all of one's change in a parking meter. I was moving so slowly that it felt like I might need to set up camp. In what seemed an instant, the peloton was rolling away from me and I was watching the backs of the follow caravan cars getting smaller. I struggled to keep the bike going forward and began thinking about the long, lonely, and boring road ahead. I was jarred back from my daydream by a loud car horn.

"Hey, get out of the way, *jongen!*" Jan Raas, the director of the Super Confex team from Holland, was screaming and trying to pass me on both sides. I moved right, and he was gone. That was it, it seemed. He was the last one. The rest of the caravan was gone, but there was no ambulance or broom wagon following me, so I figured I was abandoned in that terrible no-man's-land between racing the race and quitting the race. I kept going anyway. In these events, it was always possible that the peloton would find some reason to slow down. I caught a French rider whom I could not recognize. I didn't think we were going to catch anyone because he seemed even weaker at that point than I was, but that didn't stop me from sitting on his wheel when he was able to take his turn on the front.

All of a sudden, two gendarmes appeared from nowhere in a small, gendarmerie-blue Renault sedan. They slowed, and the one on the passenger side made the universal bike-racer-being-towed-by-a-car gesture. I answered with the universal thankful-bike-racer sigh and reached for the doorpost, but he brushed my arm off and gestured again. This time it was the index finger moving back and forth in front of his face, which meant I wasn't getting a ride just yet. That gesture was quickly followed by two fingers pointing at his eyes, followed by an index finger pointing at my face and then back at his face. This was the universal sign for "Give me your sunglasses and you can hang on to the car." I pulled the hideous Time sunglasses off my head and handed them over. I had another pair in my pocket anyway.

I was set, but even with my limited French-language skills, I figured out that my French riding partner was going to be left behind because he didn't have anything the cops wanted. I fished the other pair of sunglasses from my pocket and handed them to the cop. This pair was a slightly different color, so the two discussed the situation for a minute or two. When they finally reached an agreement as to each pair's ownership, they picked up the pace. Soon we were going 90 kph, with me hanging on to the passenger side of the police car and the French rider hanging on to the driver's side. At this rate we would probably be able to catch some larger group of riders soon. But less than 2 km into our tow, I heard the unmistakable sound of a bike and its rider sliding across the pavement. The cop behind the wheel lifted off the gas for just a moment and then put the hammer back down. The one on the passenger side looked at me and shrugged. I didn't say a word.

○ ○ ○

When we got to our hotel the evening before the last day of the race, I was anxious to get some rest. The final stage had some long climbs, and I wanted to make sure I could at least make it to the last climb with some sort of a group. We walked past six or seven men sitting on a long vinyl bench and through a curtain to the stairs that led to our rooms. Tonight I would have a new roommate because the previous morning Cocquyt had informed me that he was going home.

"I have a headache," he told me.

"What?" I asked him. "You are going home because you have a headache? Get something from *dikke* Gerard." Gerard was a soigneur who would be certain to have a remedy. He was a heavy guy, topping the scales at 350 pounds or so, which was why we called him *"dikke"* (fat) Gerard. Getting a massage from Gerard was anything but relaxing. His size meant that any physical effort caused him to wheeze and sweat profusely, with much of that sweat landing in huge drops on my legs.

"I don't think that will help because . . ." Cocquyt laughed. "I have a headache from hitting the doping lamp."

I had a hard time laughing because this was Cocquyt's second doping violation for the year. The suspended thirty-day sentence that had come with the first violation was now added to another thirty-day suspension and was due immediately. Along with the forced vacation came a serious monetary fine, one that Cocquyt didn't want to pay. Just like that, my best friend, teammate, and training partner was gone.

Eurotop was one of the lower teams on the totem pole of world professional cycling, and we were often relegated to the nastiest hotels. This was one of the worst. To begin with, there was no private bathroom; instead a shower, toilet, and sink were all located at the foot of the two double beds. These fixtures had been installed long after the building had originally been constructed and were set on a pedestal, roughly two feet above the floor. The double beds, while generous, were disgusting. Mine had a deep indentation in the center, giving me only the option of lying on my back. Most notable, though, was the fact that the sheets had not been washed in a long, long time. There was a rank smell filling the room of body odor, old socks, old cheese, cigarette smoke, and rotten cauliflower. We opened the windows, but it was no use. I climbed up into the shower and tried to wash off the day's sweat, dust, and diesel exhaust, but the water that dribbled out of the showerhead also smelled of something foul.

Trying to sleep was impossible. As soon as I started to drift off, I heard laughing women running down the halls. As an added attraction, my roommate thought he was coming down with a cold and refused to have the window open. It was the beginning of summer in the microwave of France, so the temperature in our room never dipped below the hell mark on my body's thermometer. If Cocquyt were there I would have begged him for some Ansiolin or something else for sleeping. My roommate had already fallen asleep, but I doubt he could have helped me anyway.

I was the first one at the breakfast table in the morning. Our start was not early for the final day, so I had not gotten downstairs early either; it was strange that there wasn't more activity in the hotel. This was the south of France, sure, but it was still France, not Spain, and people here didn't usually sleep late. When the people and food finally appeared, I rushed through my breakfast, opting only for packaged foods and black coffee instead of my preferred café au lait. After that I quickly got dressed, brought my bags down for *dikke* Gerard, and sat down outside on a bench in front of the hotel. I was way too early to be ready for the stage, but I'd had as much of this place as I could take.

We were halfway from the hotel to the race start when I learned we had spent the night in a whorehouse. When I was thirteen or fourteen years old, I had gotten to ride a motorcycle race from Barstow, California, to Las Vegas, Nevada. My best friend, Kurt, and I were supposed to stay in our hotel room at the Sands while our fathers went out for a beer. Instead of sitting in the room watching TV, Kurt and I left the hotel to walk on the Strip. We quickly found ourselves hanging out with a group of working girls, all dressed in flowing white. They played with my hair while Kurt impressed them with his 14-year-old biceps. Lit by the strange Las Vegas light, they were all beautiful and angelic, and I wondered why people thought prostitution was a bad thing. The women I had seen and heard in our hotel at the Midi Libre were not at all the way I had pictured hookers since my trip to Vegas years before. I decided it must just be a cultural difference. I have never been happier and more relieved to leave a hotel and get to the start of a bike race.

5

Stars and Stripes

THOUGH MY RESULTS IN 1988 WERE MEAGER BY BELGIAN STAN-
dards, they were not bad for an American pro, and I was chosen
for the team that would represent the United States at the World
Championships in Ronse, Belgium, on August 28. It would have
been a greater accomplishment, perhaps, had I been an Italian
or Belgian rider named to represent my country because the
professional rider pool in those countries is so much deeper. As
I looked at it, though, my selection was a great honor, and I was
determined to haul out the best ride I could possibly deliver.

The announcement was made far enough in advance that Albert Claeys and I were able to devise a training plan to put me in
top form for the race. The custom of the day was to train for a
race by entering other races. There were two back-to-back stage
races leading up to the world's: the Vuelta Ciclistica a Burgos
in Spain and the Tour of Belgium. I had failed miserably at the

Burgos the year before, and I was eager to get it right on my second attempt.

The team had us flying to Spain from Lille, France, just past the French-Belgian border. American citizens still needed a visa to enter France, and my passport didn't have one. I called Florent for a change of plans. I didn't want to make the drive with the mechanics, so a ticket was booked for me on a flight out of Brussels on the same day that the rest of the guys would fly from Lille. The race organization arranged for a taxi to pick me up at the airport and drive me the two hours to my team's hotel.

When I made my way past the Spanish customs agents and through the doors to the arrival area, I saw several people holding up passenger names or company signs, but nothing for me. One cabbie was holding a handwritten sign that read, "Super Confex." I thought for a minute and remembered that there hadn't been any other cycling people on my plane. Raas's riders surely would have flown out of Amsterdam. I figured the organization had just goofed up somewhere, and that was my cab, but I never did find out what the true explanation was. I held up my hand to get the driver's attention and then pointed at myself.

"Soopaireh Cone-fess?" he asked, putting down the sign.

"*Si.*"

Apparently my answer in his language signaled that I was a fluent Spanish speaker because he launched into a high-speed Spanish conversation. Unfortunately, I couldn't understand a word. I shrugged and gave him an exaggerated look of confusion.

"*Ik spreek het geen spaans,*" I told him, as if he were going to be able to understand Flemish when he couldn't understand English. I have noticed that when people cannot speak the language they should be speaking to another person, they speak the second one they know. I have no idea why. He shot back an understanding nod but kept speaking Spanish at about a hundred words per minute.

Evidently it was going to be a long drive from Madrid to Burgos—long enough that my cab driver and new friend suggested that I should sit in the front seat. I hate sitting in the back of a cab, and this was a small Spanish SEAT with no room in the backseat for my long legs, so I was happy to acknowledge his gestures and follow along. By 1988 seatbelts had been mandated for use in the front seats of vehicles in Spain, but they were not at all fashionable, so neither of us buckled up. On the road, I quickly learned of this new law because every time a cop was within a hundred meters, my cabbie gestured for me to pull the belt across my shoulder to make it look like I was in compliance. After working the belt four or five times, we were out of town and on our way to Burgos.

Every once in a while the cab driver would break into some sort of monologue, perhaps telling me his life story or how much he hated having to pick me up and take me all the way to Burgos. The little SEAT was wound out and screaming in protest at the speeds he was asking of it. It was surreal and entertaining, to say the least—a cross between an old rerun of *I Love Lucy* and a scene from *Night on Earth*. All I could do was nod.

We were halfway into the trip when the cabbie looked over and tipped his right hand to his lips as if he were quenching his thirst for the first time in months. He was looking for approval. I nodded. I had no clue where we were, and I was not about to give this guy any reason to kick me out of his cab. If he were thirsty, I would go ahead and be thirsty too.

We pulled off the road at the top of one of the many rolling hills we had been crossing since the start and stopped in front of a nondescript Spanish bar. I was used to sitting down and being served, but my cabbie was on a faster mission and ordered at the bar, posthaste. I asked for water "with gas," knowing the bubbles would most likely ensure I would get something bottled, as opposed to the sewer water I might get if I just asked for water. The bartender quickly produced a tall glass and a small bottle of sparkling water as well as a tall glass of ice half filled with Coke accompanied by a small glass full of brown liquid that I figured was whiskey. My cabbie poured the whiskey into the Coke and drained it as if it were the last 20 km of a 300-km race in which he had missed all his feeds. My lips weren't even wet when the bartender set him up with another round. By the time I was halfway done with my water, the bartender was delivering round number three. Soon after that I pulled out my wallet and produced the pesetas necessary to preclude round number six.

Back on the road, the cabbie was a little quieter and more serious about his mission. The road was straight, and there wasn't much traffic, but it was clear that it had become something of a challenge for him to negotiate. I didn't really care, as this was seemingly my best chance to get to the start of the Vuelta Ciclistica a Burgos. Every so often, I peeked out of the corner of my eye to try to get an idea of how fast we were going. I wasn't scared of the speed, but I was curious and did my best to hide my curiosity. Just as we came over the top of a 200- or 300-foot rise, I caught a glimpse of the speedometer: 140 kph.

"*Hostia!*" the cab driver yelled. It was a curse I had heard the previous year riding in Spain. A *hostia* is literally the small wafer given during a Catholic communion mass in Spain, but somehow the word has acquired a secondary meaning. I looked up and was able to throw my arms forward onto the dash to brace myself just as he hit the brakes. We were heading for what looked like a German shepherd that was walking across the road too slowly. The car slewed as the cabbie mashed the brake pedal with all his might. Under normal circumstances, he wouldn't have had to fight hard to keep the car straight, but with the five drinks in him it was a struggle. The dog stopped walking as if more interested in watching this scene unfold than in escaping. The thud when we hit the dog wasn't too loud since we had managed to slow to something less than 10 kph.

"*Hostia,*" the driver said again, this time in a pathetic tone. I craned my neck to see over the front of the car. The dog ran off into the bushes. The cabbie was already getting out of the car, seemingly yelling at the dog. Instead of trying to find out whether the dog was okay, he put his hands to his head, pointed at the front of his car, and then put his hands back on his head. I decided to take a look to see what kind of damage had been done. From the scene he was making, I suspected the whole bumper was caved in, but in fact there was nothing wrong. He pointed, gestured, and babbled inconsolably for a few more minutes and then, all at once, snapped out of it. We got back in the car and were on our way. For the rest of the trip, every few minutes he would utter something that I assumed had to do with that poor dog and the front of his cab.

● ● ●

Several days into the Vuelta a Burgos, I accidentally found myself in a breakaway that formed two-thirds into one of the hilliest stages of the race. I had been riding with the real climbers, guys who were completely familiar with the front of a mountain race.

For most of the first climb I was able to stay in the group without any trouble; the break had just formed, and nobody was going to attack yet. It was better to stay together now and duke it out later on the flat, 30-km run to the finish.

Our group was small, and we had successfully gotten enough of a gap that the team cars were able to come through to us. Florent beamed as he drove beside me. The man who had been Eddy Merckx's very first directeur sportif in the pro ranks had now been relegated to small teams without much talent in these kinds of races. I was proud to be making the old man happy.

At the sign marking 3 km to the top, the pace picked up and I slid toward the back. I counted down the inches to the next kilometer marker. At 1 km to go, the pace picked up again as the guys in our group started thinking about the king-of-the-mountains sprint. Back in the days before each team had washers and dryers in its support truck, wearing some sort of leader's jersey was as much about having to wash one less piece of clothing in your hotel bathtub or bidet as it was about the honor and prize money.

I would have loved to wear a climber's jersey just once in my career, but this was definitely not going to be my chance. I stared at the rear wheel in front of me and made every effort to keep the gap between it and my front wheel the same. At the 500-meter sign, the gap had grown to more than a bike length. I was fighting with my legs for every meter. At 200 meters to go, I was more than 10 meters from the rider in front of me, who was more than 10 meters from the rider in front of him. The sprint for king of the mountains had shattered our little group. I thought I might be watching my good race end, but once over the top I was able to catch the group after just six or eight turns on the tight descent.

I wanted to be a professional athlete practically from birth.

Here I am working on my pre-race bike-hero pose in front of my parents' house in Johnson City, Tennessee.

We were not racing at the 1991 Tour de France, so I returned to the States to train in the mountains. It was the fittest point in my career: I was carrying just 142 pounds on my 6-foot frame.

Albert and I, about three weeks
after I signed my first contract
as a professional cyclist, posing
in the Claeys family's backyard.
If I had known what I was in for,
I am sure I would have looked
more nervous.

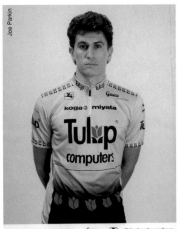

The Tulip team kit was my all-time
favorite, and having my own hero card
with this team was great. However,
waiting four hours in an unheated photo
studio during the Dutch winter
was not a bonus.

After a training ride, we did our hero card photos for Eurotop at a local Citroën dealership. This was not my bike. I was angry about it because I would never have been seen in public with dirty handlebar tape.

Joseph Parkin

Albert gives me some last-minute wisdom before the start of the 1989 Brabantse Pijl. Along with the race food, there were two Captagon tablets in my back pockets. Knee warmers had not yet been invented.

A room on the third floor of Albert and Rita's Café Sportwereld was my home in Belgium. At one point, my name was painted on the front window, signifying that the café was my supporters' club headquarters.

While this jersey was not as impressive as the USA team jersey I donned for the 1988 World Road Championship, I counted myself equally lucky to wear it at the World Professional Mountain Bike Championship in 1995.

After I returned to the States, I was lucky to make a decent living racing for Len Pettyjohn and the Coors Light team, but 1994 was the last year for Coors Light—and my last as a road racer.

The crash between Steve Bauer and Claude Criquielion at the 1988
World Road Championship was a tragic moment for both riders.
(John Pierce/PhotoSport International)

Even though I thought I was good enough to ride in the 1988 World Road
Championship race, I still needed to get my mug on TV to get some bonus
pay. In this layout from *Winning* magazine, I'm on the front in the stars and
stripes, dragging the peloton up the steep grade of the Kluisstraat just as
the Eurovision broadcast went live again for the race finish.
*(*Winning *magazine, December 1988; photo by Graham Watson)*

Cees Priem as a team director, doing what he did best: yell at riders. *(Cor Vos)*

One of the coolest riders I ever knew in one of the coolest uniforms: Patrick Cocquyt on the Koppenberg at the Tour of Flanders, 1985. No matter how cool you are, the Koppenberg often cannot be climbed on the bike. *(Graham Watson)*

Eddy Planckaert at his rightful place near the front, on Alpe d'Huez in 1989. *(John Pierce/ PhotoSport International)*

Eddy Planckaert relaxing in the green jersey before a stage of the Tour de France. Some time before, I had gone for a ride with Eddy, sporting a white-trash hairdo. Next thing I knew, he was introducing this amazing look to the pro peloton. (*Cor Vos*)

Here with the requisite Saint Christopher medal sewn to his hairnet, Fons de Wolf was a tabloid hero who was supposed to be the next coming of Eddy Merckx. *(Cor Vos)*

Fons de Wolf delivered promising results early in his career but ended it in the service of others. Still, he was usually a powerful force in the spring classics. *(Cor Vos)*

Frank Hoste was one of the nicest—and most gullible—riders I ever knew. The former green-jersey winner, here in the Tour de France in 1984, once helped me keep my white jersey of the best young rider in a minor stage race. *(John Pierce/PhotoSport International)*

By no means the most famous of team directors, José de Cauwer might be among the greatest motivators. I rode myself into a coma just because he asked me to. *(Cor Vos)*

Jules de Wever was the first director I rode for as a pro. *(Cor Vos)*

Jules de Wever, second from left, with Ti Raleigh team boss Peter Post, center, and the late Bert Oosterbosch at right. *(Cor Vos)*

Luc Roosen wore the yellow jersey in the 1991 Tour de Suisse for all but a day. A great teammate, he thanked me each evening for helping him do that. *(Cor Vos)*

Roger de Vlaeminck, Mr. Paris-Roubaix (shown here in the 1973 edition), was perhaps the last of the truly great Belgian bike racers, one who could do everything well. My flat-back racing style was often compared to his.
(John Pierce/PhotoSport International)

On the next climb I was calmer because I had now officially *raced* a bike over one of the big mountains with real climbers. The tempo was a little harder because this was the last climb, and I let myself slip back with just about 500 meters to go to the top. I lost a lot of ground on the leaders but had new confidence about being able to get them back once the road pointed down. This time I hung it out on the descent, pushing hard and taking some chances. It paid off when I made up the gap quickly, catching and dropping other riders in the process.

Once on the bottom, Florent came up next to me again and told me to go easy because Marino Lejarreta's entire Caja Rural team was chasing at the front of a fairly large group. Hearing you're being chased by an entire team is never a good thing, but this was different, as Lejarreta was a hero of mine at the time. I was almost happy to hear about the chase.

With about 20 km to go, my team car came up one more time so Florent could tell me the chase had closed to the point where the team cars would now have to pull over to let the riders pass. Since these guys had been riding faster than our group for some time now, I had to prepare for the speed to increase. The last thing a chasing team or group can allow when they catch a breakaway is for the race tempo to slow because that could allow new attacks to form. I knew I was in for an increase in the tempo, but I didn't expect it to be as violent as it was. We were caught at about the 18-km-to-go mark, and by 16 to go I was in serious trouble. The road had flattened, but I was unable to suck up behind the rider in front of me. I quickly slipped to the back. I heard the horn and knew it was Florent.

"God verdomme! God verdomme! God verdomme!" Florent had half his torso out of the car window and was banging on the

door as hard as he could. He was yelling so loudly that his voice cracked. "Stay on that wheel! Goddamn it, stay on that wheel! You *will* stay on that wheel!"

I was already feeling like my legs had gotten too short to extend to the bottom of my pedal stroke, and my arms were feeling like they might break off at the elbows. I wanted a bigger gear, but I didn't have one, and my legs didn't want to move any faster, which wasn't fast enough. I slipped off the back of the group. Florent let me ride by myself for about 2 km and then in the ultimate sign of disgust passed me with the windows rolled up.

The next morning I sat on the hood of the soigneurs' car before the start of the race. Normally I would have been hanging out near Florent and Albert, listening to their opinions on how the day would unfold, but I was still mad at Florent and didn't want anything to do with him. While he had every right to be angry with me, I didn't appreciate the public flogging.

Albert showed up a couple minutes later with Benny, the mechanic from Super Confex. It seemed that his boss had been impressed with the way I'd ridden the day before and thought I should ride with his team next year. I asked how that was possible since I had been dropped. I was told that it was the fact that I had just kept coming back; they felt it meant I had something to offer. Since the World Championships were still a few weeks away, contract negotiations with a new team weren't supposed to be under way, so it was left to casual discussion between me and the adjutant director, Hilaire van der Schueren. He offered me 1 million Belgian francs for one year—roughly $30,000. I finished fourth that day. It was a sprint finish that I remembered from the year before. I knew I had to stay near the front going into a turn just 2 km from the finish; from that point on, there were so many corners that there would be no other opportunities to pass. That night I was told that José de Cauwer, the director of the ADR team, wanted to talk to me about riding for his team. Things were starting to look up.

∘ ∘ ∘

Despite the bobble, Burgos had been really good. My form was starting to come, and, most importantly, I had some good confidence going into the Tour of Belgium. With the world's just a few weeks away, finding my form now was important. Stage races typically either build up a rider's fitness level or destroy it. I was finding that more racing was better; I was feeling stronger and more confident as each day passed. With just one day left to race, I was hanging on to 10th in the general classification.

The last stage would start and finish in the town of Leuven, home of the Stella Artois brewery. Florent was from Leuven and happy to bring home a top-ten finish from his young American, even if it wasn't a stage win or a podium place overall. Today's final stage finished with several kermis-length circuits of the town, complete with a small climb and a section of narrow, old cobblestones.

This was the first time I was poised to come away with any sort of result in a pro stage race, so I was nervous until we hit the finishing circuits and the feed zone. Feed zones are sometimes scary places, especially at the start of a set of finishing circuits or late in the race, when attacks may happen and riders are nervous.

I tried to position myself as close to the front as I could without wasting too much energy. The soigneurs were spaced along the right side of the road, as usual, with armfuls of musette bags. I was following Nico Verhoeven, and as I spotted *dikke* Gerard, I moved my left hand to the top of the handlebar, not far from the stem. If Gerard had overloaded the bags, as he sometimes did, this would help keep me from swerving all over the road as the bag tried to rip my right arm out of its socket.

I grabbed the musette, which sure enough was loaded with two full water bottles, a can of Coke, and enough food for a family picnic. My arm swung back, just as I had anticipated, but I didn't veer off course. Then I saw one of the TVM soigneurs step into Nico's path. Nico grabbed a handful of brakes—enough that his rear wheel rose off the ground by several inches. With one hand on the middle of the bars, nowhere near a brake lever, I had no way to slow down. My right hand was wrapped in the musette bag's long handle, and even though I let go of it, it stayed with me. I extended my right arm, and my hand hit Nico's back, slowing me down and pushing him forward. I was off balance, though, and hit the ground.

It was a big hit. My shorts and jersey were ripped. The handlebars on my bike were bent, and the rear brake lever was destroyed. I was sitting 10th in the Tour of Belgium and didn't want to take time to get on my spare bike, so I got back on my beat-up bike and started chasing the race. One of my teammates must have seen the crash because several of them waited to help me rejoin the peloton. It was a nice gesture, but none of them had the horsepower needed to help me in the situation. I rode past the guys as if they were standing still. I figured it was going to be important for me to get back to the front before the cobblestones. The handlebar tape had been torn and was unraveling as I rode. Several laps later, with one brake, a crooked front wheel, and bent handlebars with no handlebar tape, I stayed close enough to the front to see the final lunge for the finish line and kept my 10th place in the final standings.

∘ ∘ ∘

Bob Roll and I leaned on the top tubes of our bikes behind the start/finish line in Ronse, Belgium. In just a few minutes we would start the 1988 Professional World Road Cycling Championship. Bob was busy heckling a cameraman and a soundman from Dutch television. While I watched him, my mind flickered between the daunting task that lay ahead, the hordes of fans who were already lining the course, and the red, white, and blue stars-and-stripes jersey of the U.S. team on my back.

The first image of professional cycling I had ever seen was that of Greg LeMond during the 1983 World Championship, just before he'd won. The stars-and-stripes jersey he'd worn was the coolest-looking thing I had ever seen, and I'd known from that moment that I had to have one. Now, on the start line, the magnitude of what I was about to do was starting to sink in. It was not as though I hadn't thought about it before, but only an hour ago I had been following Greg LeMond and Andy Bishop, who were in Andy's car, down this same start/finish hill. We had arrived a little later than I thought we should have and were driving downhill. Greg kept grabbing the parking brake as Andy drove, skidding the Opel a few feet at a time.

Despite Greg's accomplishments as a cyclist, America wasn't considered any kind of world power when it came to cycling. We were still in our two-wheeled infancy, so to speak, and were the last country called to the line. It didn't matter much in a race of the world's length; we weren't going to miss out on anything starting at the back, but I think the guys at the front of the field were already getting tired of standing by the time Bob and I rolled the 20 meters or so to the back of the peloton.

After the gun went off, it was another 10 seconds before either of us even crossed the start line. I watched the whole sea of national jerseys roll up the 17 percent grade for about 1 km from the start line to the top of the Kluisstraat. At the top of the hill, when a few of the no-hopers decided to stretch their legs, my time for sightseeing was over and we began the day's work.

Classics have their own brand of nervousness, but for the most part, the classics of the 1980s flowed a certain way and the nervousness was compartmentalized. The Worlds was a completely different story, however, partly because of the more international nature of the event and partly because this was the one event of the year when we were competing for mother and country and not for a vacuum-cleaner company or some such thing.

The pace wasn't especially fast; it was just nervous. We were bumping off each other as we jockeyed for position, sort of like the run up to one of the small climbs in the classics or 10 km before a big field sprint. After a couple of laps I learned that I was more than able to stay toward the front on the climb to the finish, but on the back side of the course I was having trouble holding my position.

The course was also not conducive to peeing. In any other race of that distance, peeing would have been a breeze, as large groups of riders would have stopped en masse somewhere when the pace was easy, but that wasn't happening here. The other problem was that most of the course was lined with spectators. The part of the course that was most remote was also pretty fast. I started getting nervous about my full bladder. I had gone a couple laps more than

I wanted without peeing, and I was losing my focus. In reality the pace was probably not too fast for me to have stopped, but I didn't want to risk it. I had to pee off the bike. Unfortunately, I had never practiced that before and was even a little unsure how to proceed. I had to give it a shot anyway. I dropped to the back of the peloton. I swung my right knee out and leaned off the bike as much as possible. My wrist was keeping the front of my shorts out of the way. I waited. Nothing happened. Since I couldn't pedal, I started losing ground on the back of the peloton. Shit! I really had to go. I felt a hand on my back, giving me a push. I looked back to see an American teammate, Michael Engleman.

"Looks like you need some help," he said.

"Thanks," was all I could come up with. About the last thing in the world that would have been acceptable at the urinal in a public bathroom would have been another man's hand on my back. I assure you that in this case it was not only appropriate but also completely necessary. I successfully emptied my bladder on the streets of Ronse, as well as on my legs and shoes and parts of my bike. I didn't care. I had my concentration back, and both of us were able to rejoin the peloton with minimal effort.

From racing kermises, I had learned that marking one of the locals is a pretty good strategy. I had decided in the weeks leading up to the race that Claude Criquielion was going to be the Belgian to watch in Ronse. Claudy is from the French-speaking part of Belgium, and Ronse is a bilingual city. He had won the world's in 1984, so he knew what it would take. My plan was to watch him casually for the first three-quarters of the race, so as not to be annoying. After that the plan was to become his shadow.

With six laps to go I was firmly planted on his wheel as we came over the top of the Kluisstraat. We turned left and aimed for the last little kicker of a hill before the steep, wide descent toward the back side of the course. As we turned I felt the front wheel wash out a little bit. I hoped it was just my imagination. It wasn't; within a few hundred meters the tire was completely flat. I was riding on the rim and fighting to keep the bike from blowing off the road in the strong side-wind.

I motioned for the riders behind me to pass and moved over to the left side of the line of riders. I put my hand in the air, asking for the team car. I drifted all the way to the back of the long line, and still no one came. Pretty soon the other team cars were passing me. When the Belgian team car with Eddy Merckx approached, I even stopped pedaling for a second and prepared to stop, thinking they were stopping for me, but they kept on going. We turned left at the top of the steep, four-lane descent that took the race to the back side of the course, and still no American team car. I was now seriously off the back of the bunch and starting to panic. When we neared the right-hand turn at the bottom, they arrived. It was too late.

The guys in the team car had stopped to talk to someone at the U.S. team's pit area. The radio in the 7-Eleven team car that was being used as the U.S. National Team car was not working well, so they hadn't gotten the word from the chief commissar until well after I had asked for help.

I got the wheel change, but the team cars had all gone, so there was no caravan for me to draft through to get back up to the peloton, and the peloton was racing now. When I turned left and stared up the long finishing straight, the gap was probably three-quarters of a kilometer or more. I rode one more lap, hoping the peloton might slow down for a few minutes. I knew better, though, and pulled into our pit, ending my race.

I was not happy to be in the American team pit. The guys were dropping out left and right, and no one seemed to care. It was as if everyone had resigned himself to being nothing, a second-class cyclist, unable to compete against the world's best. It took me another couple of laps before I could change back into my street clothes.

○ ○ ○

A collective gasp filled Belgium when Criquielion tangled with Steve Bauer and hit the foot of a crowd-control barrier, sending Claudy to the ground. I watched the gasp form from a couple hundred meters or so past the finish line and felt it as it exploded past me. One of the most poignant images from my era of cycling was the photo of a confused and heartbroken Criquielion on one side of the frame and a dejected Bauer on the other. Maurizio Fondreist celebrated his victory, but that victory was overshadowed by the crash that had allowed him to win.

That image yanks the breath from my lungs each time I see it. It is not only the historic image of that race's finish but also a bitter-sweet reminder of my own lost race. My palmarès, or lack thereof, would seem to suggest that history wouldn't have been much different without the flat, but I honestly believe that that should have been my day, my career's big tipping point. Nevertheless, it was one of three opportunities I have had to pull on the stars and stripes in a world championship competition, something that makes me luckier than most.

6

A Dog in a Hat

ALBERT AND I MET WITH JOSÉ DE CAUWER TO TALK OVER A CON-
tract with ADR for 1989. We still had the Super Confex offer in
our pocket, and we'd had conversations with several other teams,
but Albert liked the ADR program best. Looking back, I think he
knew there was no way for him to be head mechanic with Super
Confex because his friend Benny held that position already. Besides that, the politics on the Dutch team would most likely have
been a problem for me, just as they had been at TVM. Now, at
ADR, José presented me with an offer of 800,000 Belgian francs,
roughly $25,000, for one year.

"I was offered a million by Super Confex," I told him.

"Yes," José replied, "but this is not what we are talking about. I
am not going to negotiate against Raas."

Right away I liked José. I hadn't interacted with him much previously, but I had a good feeling about him. His comment came
with a cocky grin.

"If I ride for you, I need to have two years," I told him. Admittedly, pushing for the extra season didn't make much sense, as I was planning on winning a bunch, or at least doing well enough to make my value increase. Why lock myself into a contract that destined me to make lesser wages for two years instead of just one? It was a matter of pride. True, I needed some security, but mostly I felt that valuable riders had multiple-year deals and I wanted to be treated like one. José agreed to a two-year deal.

Next was the question of which team I would ride with. In 1988 ADR had fielded a huge team with too many riders. This would have been fine if the team had the finances to put squads in several different countries at once, but it didn't. Too many riders from one team in a kermis race simply spelled disaster, as infighting usually meant another team could steal the win.

For 1989 there would be an A team and a B team. To make the division more palatable for prospective riders, the B team was being touted as a small stage race team for the development of young riders. I liked small stage races and definitely wanted to get better as an overall racer. The A team would have me fighting to get a spot in the selection for the big races all the time and would probably also mean a steady diet of kermis races. The B team promised me the chance to do tons of little stage races and avoid the kermises. In addition, we discussed the possibility of my switching to the A team halfway through the season if I wanted to. I didn't need to sleep on it and agreed to ride for the B team. We shook hands on the deal and signed the papers a few days later.

When I returned from the States, things were not as rosy as I had expected. The team had struggled to find a title sponsor for its second squad. Greg LeMond had been hired for the A squad, which was a good thing, but so had some other riders who I thought didn't fit the bill. Although I had agreed to ride on the second squad, it had been presented a bit differently than it now appeared. We were going to be saddled with a bunch of first-year pros who, I figured, were buying their way onto the team—agreeing to be paid only a small fraction of the minimum wage by giving the difference back to the team in advance. In addition, there were two old guys who were stuck with our miserable band only because there was still a year remaining on their contracts. Luc Colijn and the late Dirk Wayenberg were salt-of-the-earth riders whom I respected, but I didn't feel that they fit the role of mentor.

Since the ADR program was essentially one big entity, both teams shared the same presentation banquet for the sponsors and press. Some of our early training sessions were done together as well. The guys on the A team had new team clothing, while those of us on the B team were dressed in whatever we had from our various previous teams. On my new team, there was a grand total of five guys out of the more-than-twenty-man squad who weren't a complete embarrassment. I knew I had made some mistakes when I'd crossed over to the big leagues, but at least I could pedal my bike.

I believed most of these guys must have used copious amounts of drugs during their careers as amateurs. They appeared to be kermis specialists in training. What was worse, I was starting to get the feeling that the team was going to focus only on lo-cal races, with perhaps the odd trip to Holland. This meant that Spanish, Italian, and French were languages I wouldn't get to hear much anymore, and I wouldn't be seeing the hillier racing that went with them. We were the ADR program's redheaded stepchildren, and I hated every minute of it.

My parents came to visit me in the spring and were able to catch the Brabantse Pijl (Flèche Brabanconne in Flemish) and the Three Days of de Panne. My dad, who traveled often for work, had amassed enough frequent-flyer miles to allow them to fly first class to London. After a night in London they took the ferry from Dover across the water to Oostende, where I picked them up. I had been able to find them a new little hotel in the neighboring town of Aalter. Having them come was a mixed blessing. On the one hand, they were my parents, and I wanted them to see me in my element. On the other hand, I was having a hard time finding my element that year. Nonetheless, I was anxious to have my dad see the races, since he was more skeptical and less appreciative of my career than my mom.

Entertaining friends and family while you're trying to race is difficult in every situation, but we had the added hurdles of language, culture, and undiagnosed illness. Not long after this trip, my dad was diagnosed with Alzheimer's disease. He was already displaying many of the symptoms, but his young age of 52 kept doctors from making the correct evaluation. My mom was nearing her wits' end; in fact, she had been hovering in that area for some time before their trip. My dad had been having a hard time speaking for a while, and most of our conversations were one-sided, with him mostly just agreeing with whatever my mom and I had said. I think she had already learned to speak on his behalf to a great extent.

I'd been able to borrow an old Audi 80 from a friend for my parents' visit because I still didn't have my own car. I used Albert's car on occasion and had driven various team box vans back from races when he'd decided to have a few beers before we left, so I was familiar with the Belgian roads and style of driving. My dad was scared to death when I was behind the wheel, and before each trip he'd ask if he could drive instead.

I was able to make it to the start of the Brabantse Pijl without killing anyone and left my mom and dad to fend for themselves while I got dressed with the rest of the team. The weather was near perfect for April in Belgium, so it should have been a good race for me to find the finish. I wasn't riding well enough to finish with a great result, but I didn't see any reason why I couldn't ride well enough to make myself happy.

Albert and my director, Patrick Versluys, thought otherwise; they thought this was the perfect opportunity for me to do something extra, especially now that my parents had arrived. I was handed two Captagon wrapped in aluminum foil and instructed to take one before the start and one if I felt I was going to make it into the final. Captagon is the brand name for fenethylline, a stimulant that affects the body in a way similar to amphetamine. I didn't know exactly what it was, but I did know it was on the doping list, and I had heard teammates talk about it as somewhat weak. Nevertheless, they spoke of it in the same breath as the hard-core amphetamines. If it had been some sort of caffeine concoction or even a pill for late-race cramps, I would have nonchalantly slid the goods into my jersey pocket. But this was different. I winced in protest.

"I don't know," I whined. "There's control here."

They didn't care about the doping control. If I were picked to be tested after the race, they'd find a way around my getting caught. I didn't feel like raising the clean-bike-racer flag, so I stuffed the drugs into my pocket. The European teams of that era (in Belgium especially) didn't think highly of goody-two-shoes riders. Like the vaunted Blue Code of Silence among police, pro bike racing definitely had the Lycra Code of Silence. I suspect that code is still strong today.

As an American I stuck out enough, so I didn't need to give anybody cause for concern, especially as poorly as I was riding. Many of the team managers, teammates, friends, and fans I had while living Belgium would have looked at *not* taking the drugs as a failure to give 100 percent to being a cyclist, and I didn't want to suddenly find myself left at home for every race because I openly refused to try. I got back on my bike and rolled over to my mom and dad.

I was now faced with a decision: Eat the Captagon as prescribed and most likely ride well but risk the doping control, or forget it and hope for the best. I was a conscientious objector and willful abstainer, but I was not a drug virgin, which made the decision a bit more difficult. The year before I had made the split in a small semiclassic in the Ardennes. I wasn't riding well, and I was feeling even worse. My stomach was killing me, and the tempo in the group was not helping matters. I was fighting with the bike for all I was worth, wishing I had never made it into this stupid front group. The team car showed up to find out how I was feeling. Usually I was able to muster some kind of casual complaint about a specific issue, but this time "I feel shitty" and "stomach" were the only words I could form. I was handed a small bottle, about half the size of a half-pint hip flask for booze and made of plastic.

"This will help," Florent told me. "Not too much—just half now, half later if you want it."

Part of me wanted to believe that those guys somehow had a small pharmacy on board that would fix my stomach. Most of me knew I was getting ready to take off my party dress. I yanked out the cork with my teeth in a style that has been passed down through generations of my hard-drinking ancestors and drank from the flask. I tasted Coca-Cola, Champ (a syrupy sugar drink), and something chalky. Maybe they had just given me something for my stomach after all, I thought. My tongue pushed the chalky particles out from between my teeth as I rode back toward the front of the group. The Coke was helping my stomach.

The temperature was in the middle to upper 70s, warm by Belgian standards, but goose bumps were beginning to form on my legs along with a strange sheen from the sweat that looked like baby oil to me. My position on the bike went from hunched over and fighting to upright and relaxed. Within minutes after I had consumed half of the little flask, I was riding at the front of the group, climbing with my hands resting comfortably on the top of the handlebars, close to the stem. It felt as if the tempo had slowed, and I looked back to see what was going on. I felt that someone would surely be attacking at any moment because the pace was so slow. I looked back again. Many of the other riders in the group were fighting with their bikes, as I had been doing just a few minutes before.

"What is wrong with these people?" I wondered out loud to myself.

If we continued riding so slowly, I was sure we were going to get caught. I started upping the tempo, ever so slightly. We approached the finishing circuits, so I knocked back the rest of the contents of the flask. I made sure to put the thing back in my pocket instead of throwing it to the side of the road. I didn't want anyone to sample the contents. After the finish line and some right and left turns, there was a short climb out of town. On the first passage of this climb I made sure to position myself toward the front and then fought back the urge to take the lead. On the second climb of the same hill, I was no longer able to control my energy. I went to the lead and set the tempo. I looked back as former Tour de France stage winners, classics winners, and other notable bike racers were put into trouble by the pace. All the while I was sitting comfortably on my bike, practically breathing through my nose.

When we made it to a lap and a half to go, Corneille Daems made an offer to the seven or eight riders still in the breakaway for him to win the race. I cannot remember the amount he proposed, but it was pretty good, good enough for most of the rest of them. But I was feeling too strong.

"*Non.*" I waved him off. "*Nee.*" After one or two more turns through the pace line Edwig van Hooydonk approached me, pushing his freckled face toward mine.

"You want to win?" he asked accusingly and shot me a glare as if I had just asked to sleep with his wife.

"*Ja,*" I answered. But we were cut short as Daems attacked and the rest of the group chased him.

I had heard a lot of the old Belgians use the expression, "*een hond met een hoed op,*" which means "a dog with a hat on." In the context in which I heard it, I took it to mean that you see a dog in a hat when a normal situation changes, when something looks out of place. When instructing a young rider to control the race by reacting early and often to other teams' attacks, a director might tell the rider to look for a dog with a hat on.

In my state, I could see the hat before the dog even decided to put it on. In fact, I could see what color underwear the dog was wearing. I'm pretty sure Superman could leap tall buildings and see through walls and all that because he was jacked to the gills on amphetamine. I was countering my competitors' attacks even before they thought about making them. I was inflicting excruciating pain on every inch of my body, but I didn't care. It was amazing!

Unfortunately, each of my new strengths was outweighed by the fact that I was also becoming more stupid by the second. In reacting to my competitors before they could even attack, I was doing more work than I needed to. I was controlling the race in such a way that it was actually easier on them. If we'd been racing in Las Vegas, I would have been the drunk at the poker game trying to go all-in on a pair of twos after showing everyone else my cards.

Van Hooydonk attacked and went clear. He won. I studied the situation and somehow figured out that I was no longer going to win and, that being the case, should stay off the podium to lessen the odds of being sent to doping control. Most medical controls are limited to the top three riders, plus two random picks. Usually the rest of the top 10 finishers are not included in the random selection and this race was no exception.

I was still supernatural well into the night. I was up early the next morning and went to ride off my hangover. Plodding along at a slow speed was about all I could handle, so I stayed perched on my bike for most of the day. The day after that I went to a kermis race. I can't remember if this was one I was supposed to ride or if I thought it would be good to blow the legs out a bit, but the extra effort I had been able to expend a couple days before had taken its toll. I am sure it was partly perception, since the race had come so easily when I was doped, but as well as I knew my body, I knew I had done a good job of hurting it.

A doctor once told me that a well-trained athlete can find about 85 percent of his potential, whereas a well-trained athlete on amphetamines will be able to perform at 105 percent. Whether or not that could be proven didn't matter to me because I was feeling the aftereffects in this kermis race. I dropped out at about the two-hour mark, determined that this was going to be the last time I would feel this way.

○ ○ ○

As I waited for the start of the Brabantse Pijl, the ill effects of the doping the year before were mostly sequestered in the far recesses of my mind. Instead, I remembered being Superman. Still, I didn't want anything to do with the Captagon tablets. If I had a saving grace, it was the fear of being the first American to get popped for doping. I couldn't stand the thought. Perhaps it was a weak crutch, but it was the one I was leaning on, and it worked for me. I also thought about how the doping controls were being beaten at the time: catheters filling the rider's bladder with "clean" urine or modified condoms placed in other orifices and then filled with "clean" urine. Those were the two that stuck out, but there were a host of others.

I could almost see a bad television sitcom flashback scene, with me lying on a table wearing a former Kentucky Derby winner's victory wreath while a fat Belgian soigneur helped get me ready to beat the control. After a loud knock a blond stripper dressed like a nurse would appear and open the door. My parents would be standing on the other side, hoping to come in and congratulate me on my win.

"Oh, hi," the nurse would say, giggling and pointing at me. "Joe can't come to the door right now 'cause that fat man is shoving a condom in his butt. Hee hee."

Imaginary sitcom nightmare or not, I didn't want to see the expressions on my parents' faces or feel the pain on mine. About halfway through the Brabantse Pijl, I knew I was not going to take the pill I had been supposed to take at the start. A little while later, after struggling with the decision to avoid the second pill as well, I realized that I wasn't paying attention to the race at all. In fact, I was no longer in the first group. On the second or third finishing circuits, I turned left and headed for the showers.

I looked my bosses in the eyes and told them that what they had given me hadn't worked and, in fact, had blocked my legs. For some reason they bought it. More importantly, I was able to meet my parents' eyes when I explained that it just hadn't been my day. At that moment in time, looking them in the face while they felt sorry for me was better than staring at their shoes while they offered their congratulations.

○ ○ ○

The Three Days of de Panne mimicked the year I was having; I was not quite there. Fortunately, it was a stage race, so I was actually making it to the finish of each stage. De Panne is a great final warm-up for the windy, flat, and fast Flanders classics that follow it. The finishing circuit on the final day of the race was one of my favorites despite the fact that I was not a sprinter and never had any hope of a great result. The circuit is dead flat with right-hand turns. The final turn is greater than 90 degrees, and the final dash to the line is a bit narrower than the rest of the course. True to Belgian form, the finish straight is on small, smooth cobblestones.

With just over two laps to go, I saw my sprinter teammate Johan de Vos raise his hand. His front tire was going flat. Our team car was toward the back of the caravan because we had no one placed highly in the general classification, so I swung to the right of the peloton and grabbed a handful of brakes. Johan was now riding slowly on the front rim, and I yelled at him to stop. I jumped off my bike, released my front wheel, and threw the bike on the ground. Johan had his front wheel off by this point. We managed to get mine stuffed up into his front fork, and I pushed him as his feet found the pedals. He was nearly up to speed and drafting his way back through the caravan when our car got to me. Albert was out of the car and had me fixed before the car was even at a complete stop.

My dad had been in the passenger seat of our team car since the start that day, so I looked back to make sure he was still there. He had an expression that bordered on panic; his eyes were wide and his jaw was tight. I suppose now that some of what I was seeing was confusion caused by the Alzheimer's, but I would like to think that some of it was because he was getting to live the moment with me.

They caught me again as I was winding my way back up through the follow cars. Albert usually liked to work on the back brake for a while before his returning rider made the final jump from the lead follow car to the back of the peloton. It was a way for the rider to rest a bit because Albert's shoulder would be pushing the bike as he worked. Since we were in full final race mode, there wasn't time for him to do that. I looked off to my left and saw my dad waving me forward. He had that same expression on his face. I smiled at him, laughed even, and then made the jump across to the back of the peloton. Despite our best efforts, De Vos was only third or fourth or something in the sprint, but I got to show my dad my element.

● ● ●

Our B team had not yet been out of Belgium when we got an invitation to the late-spring Giro del Trentino in Italy. Even this didn't cheer me up. Trentino, while by no means the hardest race on the calendar, is still much more than a flat kermis race, and most of the Italians would be riding well by this time of the year.

The ADR A squad flew almost everywhere, but our squad, which now had the title sponsor Humo, a Belgian entertainment and gossip magazine, rode the ADR tour bus. Although that may seem like a rock-star fantasy come true, it was actually a living hell. The two-story bus seemed purpose-built for a bike race team, complete with a massage table, airline-style reclining chairs, and sleeping "tubes." Unfortunately, the bus driver would not allow sleeping in these special compartments, nor would he allow us to lie on the massage table. Instead he kept it stacked with luggage and boxes. The bathroom was only open some of the time. The video monitors, when they worked, played the two porno movies the team had in its inventory—one black-and-white and in French and the other something from America. I have never understood the attraction of a group of guys watching porn together, and when they watch the same porn together over and over again, I think there might be something wrong. The porn would play, the upper deck of the bus would getter hotter by the minute, and despite my best efforts, everyone but me would reject the air conditioning. I found that I could crank open the air vent on the top of the bus and stand on a suitcase to catch some fresh air. I spent the entire fifteen-plus-hour trip to Italy alternating between standing on the suitcase with my head in the breeze like a dog and sitting behind the bus driver on a bench, secretly wishing I could kill him.

As I had anticipated, racing the Giro del Trentino was too much for me, and I found myself riding with the last groups. After a few days I climbed into one of our cars at a feed zone. I spent the rest of my time in Italy riding by myself, slowly. For the return trip I was able to buy a box of Ansiolin from a pharmacy. I ate three so I could survive the trip home in a state of blissful contempt.

This scenario was repeated at the Midi Libre; something needed to change. I called and asked my mom to read through *VeloNews* to try to find some races I might be able to do in the States. Part of me needed an excuse to go home. I talked it over with Albert and Versluys, explaining that I wanted to return to the United States to find some form somewhere. I showed them that there were some small stage races in the mountains that I could do. I argued that this trip was basically at Tour de France time anyway, so I would only be missing the kermis races. I reminded them that I had originally been told that the team would not require me to do any kermis races. I reminded them that I was being groomed as a stage racer. I won the argument, not that it took much effort, and booked a flight to Denver, where my parents were living. Since I was under 24, I was able to buy student tickets and leave within three days of booking.

The day after planning my trip to the States, I came back from a five-hour training ride and, as was my custom, cleaned up and then sat down for some coffee and a sandwich or two of cheese and jelly. I finished my lunch, poured myself one more cup of coffee, and put my feet up on one of the kitchen chairs. Since it was nearly summertime in Belgium, the kitchen door was open, and through the screen I saw the local police officer climb off his bike and walk toward the door. That was a bit odd, since the kitchen door was not the business end of the house. He knocked on the door.

"*Ja,*" I said.

"I have some papers for you," he told me, in Flemish.

"*Voor mij of Albert?*" I asked. For me or Albert? I opened the screen door.

"For you," he replied and handed me the document.

I skimmed the words and stuck on the part that stated, "72 hours to leave Belgium." I was being deported. I was stuck between disbelief and an incredible desire to laugh in his face.

"You have to sign here," he told me, pointing to the paper. He handed me his pen, and I obliged him.

"This is funny." I laughed. "How long have you seen me here?"

"A year or two, for sure," he replied.

"Or three," I corrected. "I have been here for three years, paying at least 50 percent of my salary to Belgium. This year I asked for them to let me live here legally. I guess I shouldn't have done that."

He shrugged and took back the document and his pen. Then he handed me one of the carbon copies.

"I have to come back in three days to make sure you have left," he told me.

"It's okay," I assured him, holding out my hand. "I have already booked a ticket to go back to America. Good luck for me, eh?"

After a year and a half of living in Belgium without the proper documentation, I had decided to apply for a temporary residence visa and a work permit. I was told the work permit was required before I would be granted the temporary residence visa. I registered with the local government and began the process of doctor's exams and paperwork and buying high-priced stamps to affix to each new document. It took a lot of time and a reasonable amount of money to get the whole application completed. A few weeks before the constable's visit, I had received a letter from the Belgian government refusing to grant me residency and permission to work.

As a cyclist racing for a Belgian team, I fell into a strange void because no one was claiming me as an employee. The money came from the team, but it was not the one signing my check, so it was not legally allowed to call me an employee without giving me a job as a mechanic or something. In Belgium at that time, three months' salary for each rider had to be placed into an escrow account with the Belgian Cycling Federation before the team would be granted a license. After that, monthly deposits to cover the riders' salaries had to be submitted to the federation, and it in turn made the automatic deposits into each rider's bank account.

When I was told that the team was not really my employer, I argued that the Belgian Cycling Federation must be my employer. Since no one was taking the credit for giving me a job, the government decided I was unemployed. Belgium felt that if it gave me a work permit and then a temporary residence visa, I would be able to take potential work away from one of its citizens. The funny part is that if an employer had actually taken credit for giving me a job, I would have been okay. In other words, Belgium simply didn't want to give me permission to come looking for work. I vowed to carry on as an illegal alien for the rest of my career.

∘ ∘ ∘

They say you can't go home again. I think they are right. I did not enjoy racing in America during my break. My brother Jay, my parents, and I took off for the Casper Classic stage race in Casper, Wyoming. The culture shock could not have been more intense. I was accustomed to the disciplined and uniform manner in which the European races unfolded, and what I saw in Wyoming was pure chaos. In Europe the riders almost always remained completely calm, never raising their voices to each other. Here riders screamed at each other, screamed at the fans, screamed at me. In Belgium, even for the lowliest of amateur kermis races, the officials wore suits. The riders removed their hats when in the presence of an official. Here it seemed that the officials were serving some sort of terrible community service sentence, as they had nothing but contempt for the riders.

The prologue was a 1-km uphill sprint. Despite feeling like I was swimming in sand, I finished fourth and was the last rider to cover the distance in less than 2 minutes. I began to think about the next stage, a circuit race that I thought would be similar to the kermis races I had been doing since my arrival in Belgium. I began that race the same way I would a kermis race, near the front and going with each of the early moves to make sure I did not miss an early split of the field were it to happen. This race, though, seemed to flow slowly, as if the riders were tired from months of back-to-back racing and had made an agreement to go easy on each other until the last half of the race. There were some token attempts and some breakaways, but each time I took my turn at the front of those little groups I found myself riding away from the guy on my wheel.

I couldn't figure out what was wrong. I was not riding that well, and I certainly wasn't riding that hard when I took those turns. If I had learned one thing in Europe, it was that in order to make a breakaway work, the riders in it need to ride hard, but all accelerations need to be smooth. I know I was being smooth, so it seemed to me that the other guys just didn't feel like racing that hard.

What was even stranger was that it wasn't the big teams controlling the flow of the race but the small ones and some individual riders. These underdogs were making it even easier for the bigger teams to win. I puzzled over the rhyme and reason, or lack thereof, of American bike racing for the remainder of the stage race. I was not riding well enough to do anything spectacular, but unfortunately the pace was never hard enough to beat some form into my legs. I had only been in the States for a few days, but I was already homesick for Belgium.

o o o

A few weeks later, with my little trip nearing its end, my brothers, my parents, and I went to have some dinner and then went to a movie. Though never a big fan of Chinese food, I agreed with the choice to hit the Chinese restaurant within walking distance of my family's house. I ate most of my dinner and walked the boxed leftovers home. We headed off to the movie theater, where each of my family members chose a movie-theater snack to munch on during the show. I was still operating in bike racer mode, so I felt the need to abstain, but I was also feeling a little sick to my stomach. The pain became intense enough to draw me off the plot of the movie less than halfway through. As soon as we got home, I told my mom I wasn't feeling well and climbed into bed. All through the night I tossed and turned and sweated, wishing I could puke. At about six in the morning the burning pain that had engulfed most of my gut began to concentrate itself below my belly button and then walked its way right.

"Hey, Mom, I think my appendix is blowing up."

It was Sunday morning, so we went to the local urgent care facility. The doctors there agreed and sent me to the hospital. I was going to have to have surgery. Shit. Anesthesia was said to be really bad for a rider's form, which meant the meager gains I had made in my fitness level were now worthless. My mom drove me to Swedish Hospital and checked me in.

This particular Sunday was also the final stage of the 1989 Tour de France, and we had been following Greg LeMond's miraculous comeback as much as we could without the Internet and the daily television coverage that we have grown accustomed to today. There was network television coverage on the weekends, so my mom and I prepared for the Tour's broadcast slot as we waited for the surgeon to arrive. We watched the show's recap of prior days and laughed at the explanations the commentators aimed at the noncycling fans in the audience. And then the race came on, and we were following Greg from behind and high above, as if the camera operator was riding on the roof of a follow vehicle like a wing-walker from an old barnstormer act. I was rendered speechless. What I was seeing was magic. Those moving images of LeMond racing down the Champs Élysées toward the time trial's finish are more vivid in my mind than almost any other thing I can remember.

"He's flying!" I managed finally. My mom agreed, but I didn't think anyone but another pro cyclist could fully comprehend what we were witnessing.

Thanks to commercials and the soap-opera editing of the broadcast, the final stage of the Tour was still playing on TV when the nurses came to get me. I wouldn't find out that Greg had won until after I came out of anesthesia. It's funny that lying in a hospital bed in Englewood, Colorado, is as close as I ever came to being part of a Tour de France victory. I felt amazingly proud, as I am sure many Americans have felt over the years watching other Americans win the Tour, be they teammates, half-teammates, family, fellow cyclists, cancer survivors, or whatever. It was different this time for me because I knew so many of Greg's teammates, and I knew José. Fueled by this feeling, I was up and out of my bed less than two hours after coming out of surgery, walking the halls and talking about getting back on my bike. My doctor cut the idea short, however, telling me I would not be allowed to race for the rest of the year.

7

Through the Tulips

TO SAY THAT I WAS ANXIOUSLY AWAITING MY RETURN TO BELGIUM and the upcoming season after a five-month recovery from surgery to remove my appendix would be an incredible understatement. I was champing at the bit. I wanted so badly to be back on those roads again, riding in the rain again, that I could taste the centuries-old road grime.

I left my parents' home in Colorado two days after Christmas so that I could start training in Belgium before New Year's. I had been riding through the fall, but there was no real structure to my hours on the road, and I felt like I needed some honest Belgian bad weather to torture me back into shape. I needed to have a good year. I was entering my fourth professional season, and I was hoping to finally live up to the promise Jules de Wever had seen when he'd offered me my first contract.

Instead of flying back to Brussels, I bought a ticket to Amsterdam. Albert and I had agreed that it would be better for me to arrive in Holland than Belgium because of my recent deportation. I doubt arriving in a different Benelux country really mattered, but the plan had a cloak-and-dagger aura of subterfuge that was kind of fun.

I had been able to keep up on a lot of the gossip, rumors, and legitimate team news through frequent telephone conversations with Albert, but after picking me up at Amsterdam's Schiphol Airport, and with two and a half hours to kill on the drive home, he was able to give me all the details. He was extra-enthusiastic about the new season. Thanks to LeMond's amazing victory in the ADR colors, there had been contract talks with several multinational corporations who were willing to back the new Tour de France champion's team. The problem was that the Tour de France champ's plans for 1990 didn't involve our previously underfunded Belgian team, since he had moved to the French Z team.

Without LeMond there was no giant multinational sponsor, and without the sponsor the big-name riders started to disappear from our roster. Eddy Planckaert was the last of the superstars to leave. I had met Eddy a few times during the previous two years when my training rides had crossed paths with his. The first time this happened, there were probably ten or fifteen of us on the ride, and Eddy paired off with me immediately after finding out that I was American.

"What kind of guns do you have?" he asked.

"Uh, I have a shotgun," I said. "It was my father's when he was a kid."

"But do you not have pistols?" he asked. "You are an American; you must carry pistols."

"I don't have any pistols." I was doing my best not to laugh.

"But why would you not have pistols? If I was an American, I would have pistols. You have shoot them, eh?"

I started to wonder if I should be embarrassed, as if I had lived my entire life next to the Smithsonian or the Louvre but never set foot inside.

The truth was that my father, though not a hunter, was an expert with any weapon you put in front of him. Once when I was thirteen or fourteen, we were out in the Mojave Desert racing motorcycles, and my best friend's dad had brought his Colt 1911 and a bunch of .45-caliber ammunition. Everyone took turns shooting at the various empty jugs and bottles we had amassed over the course of the weekend. Los Angeles firefighters and cops and other assorted tough guys in the crowd all took their best shot at killing the assortment of empties. None of them had impressive weapons skills. Then my dad, the businessman, was handed the pistol. His first shot went wide—a miss. His second shot took the cap off an empty Ernest & Julio Gallo wine jug. The third shot took another couple inches off the poor bottle's neck. His fourth shot was so perfectly placed at the jug's center that nothing was left standing. That was apparently enough for him because he removed the round from the gun's chamber, made it safe, and then handed it back to its owner. He told me later that he didn't really see any need to have guns around because he was no longer in the U.S. Marine Corps.

"No, I never shot any pistols," I confessed to Eddy.

"Hoh," he grunted, making it clear that he had no more use for me.

∘ ∘ ∘

We were supposed to be teammates this year, so I rode to Eddy's house one morning with another member of the '89 Tour de France team, Phillip van Vooren, also known as "Cheepah." We arrived a few minutes after nine to find that Eddy was still in bed. The Planckaerts had a beautiful old farmhouse complete with a wood-burning stove that they still used for cooking. It was a typical Flemish winter morning, cold and damp, so stepping inside the kitchen to stand by the fire was a welcome break after the thirty-minute ride.

Eddy's wife, Christa, was still in her long red robe. Van Vooren asked if she would please get Eddy up, but she didn't want to. She said if we wanted him up, we would have to get him out of bed on our own. Van Vooren laughed and then tiptoed away to rouse our sleeping teammate.

Eddy's last ride had been sometime in early November. It was now January. When he finally graced us with his presence, he was still half asleep. We waited while he had something to eat and drink. His shoes were mismatched because neither he nor Christa could find the mates to the two shoes he dragged into the kitchen. Luckily, they were both the same style. His bike was equally neglected and caked in months-old mud. The chain was being eaten by rust. I was amazed by the nonchalance of this former green jersey winner, a former Ronde van Vlaanderen champion.

Eddy was tired, so Van Vooren and I were delegated to do the pacesetting while Eddy sat out of the wind behind us. He didn't like my speed. He wanted to go either faster or slower. A few minutes after we started, he attacked us, and Van Vooren started laughing and told me to watch. Less than a minute after the attack, Eddy was back with us, cursing his bike, his legs, the food he had just eaten, the cold, everything. A few minutes after that, he told us he couldn't ride with us anymore because we were simply going too fast. He warned us that it was too early to be going so hard. For the record, I was soft-pedaling a 42x16 just enough to make my Avocet register 25 kph. You can ride five miles in any direction from Eddy's house and the only hill you will find is a canal bridge.

It would have been fun to have been Eddy's teammate for more than a couple of days. To me there is no better embodiment of a Belgian cyclist. He was no Merckx by any stretch of the imagination, but he was a simple person who knew how to make a bike go forward really fast and hard. He knew how to find holes between other cyclists that didn't actually exist in order to make his way to the front of a sprint. Eddy was able to make his body go hard when it didn't want to. He knew that for every bit of suffering that he was putting himself through, others were suffering just as much, if not more. Most importantly, almost everything for Eddy was a game and as such was treated with typical easygoing Flemish good humor.

○ ○ ○

With no current superstars remaining on our roster, our newly rechristened IOC-Tulip team continued to train toward some sort of season, but it wasn't clear what kind of season it would turn out to be. I gravitated toward the veterans, Fons de Wolf and Frank Hoste, who would be my roommates when we traveled. I continued to dislike and distrust many of the younger riders in much the same way that I would dislike the Americans when I made it back to the States. They had a strange, nervous energy that made them incapable of riding next to another bike without half-wheeling—

keeping their wheel just in front of the other rider's in order to continuously increase the pace—yet they lacked the competitive fortitude to ride their partner into complete submission.

Training with a Dutch or Belgian team is very much a matter of showing your worth so that you can find your way into the selection for whatever race, or series of races, you want to be picked for. We rode in two single-file lines, side by side, *twee op twee,* with each pair at the front holding their spot for exactly 10 minutes—not a second more or less. I was determined to select my partners wisely and chose to start the ride next to one of the older guys whenever I could. However, there was almost never an even number of riders on our team training rides, so after a first stint on the front, the perfect pairing was usually upset and I'd find myself next to one of the guys I didn't like. I always let my veteran partners dictate the pace and felt that anyone who was my junior should allow me the same courtesy. Most of them didn't see it that way, though. To counter this lack of respect, I almost always lifted the tempo as high as I knew I could hold for the 10-minute stints. If my partner brought more speed to the table, I would reach deep into my cross-eyed reserves and raise their bet. I would keep going until the other guy blew up, came apart, and was unable to continue riding with me at the front—the bike racer version of crying "uncle."

While this was not necessarily making me popular with my teammates, some of the older guys and José were becoming more and more impressed with my ability to make others suffer. The torture was taking its toll on my body, though. I had gotten into the habit of having my blood checked every four to five weeks just to make sure everything was in good order. Red blood cells and testosterone levels have a tendency to diminish rapidly in endurance athletes, and I was more prone to these afflictions than others.

This year it wasn't so much the red blood cells as it was the testosterone. My testosterone level decreased from 8,000-something units at the first of the year to less than 3,500 units by the beginning of February. Dr. Ryckaert told me I needed to shorten the interval between blood tests, so two weeks later we tested again and found the level had dropped to roughly 1,500. Ryckaert told me I needed to take it easy, so I restricted my training to team training days. I would ride for only an hour per day on the four other days of the week. A week later I was at 700. The week after that I had the testosterone level of a seven-year-old boy.

The good doctor wanted me to stop riding completely for two weeks and rest. He explained that I was doing too much damage to my body and needed to reverse the trend. He gave me an injection of Pregnyl and ordered me to cease all training until we saw some better numbers. Pregnyl is a drug made from the urine of pregnant women and is believed to help the body produce testosterone. It had been on the list of banned substances in professional cycling for a long time but was difficult to detect so was obviously quite widely abused. As long as the rider was able to keep his testosterone level below the acceptable limit and didn't bring the empty vial into the doping control, he was safe. In my case, Dr. Ryckaert believed it was necessary to quickly reverse my rapidly decreasing testosterone level. Since I would be getting only one dose and would not be competing for some time, I felt justified in agreeing to take it.

As luck would have it, the team was not going to be training together for a while anyway, so I was able to recover while staying in my bosses' good graces. One of the most shocking double standards in professional cycling at that time was that although doing whatever it took to win was more or less encouraged, a rider using any sort of banned substance during the preseason for a training camp or team training rides was strictly frowned upon. I didn't think anyone would learn of my malady, but being able to keep to myself for a while was a lucky break. Within a month I was able to train hard again, and my testosterone level had crept back up to the region between 4,000 and 5,000. At the time the most common testing protocol set the upper limit at 10,000 units. "Normal" levels as indicated on blood-test printouts were between 3,000 and 8,000.

o o o

José was able to get us a lot of decent race contracts, and I benefited from the fact that he knew I would never fall outside the time limit of any stage race. As a result, I was selected for pretty much anything I wanted to go to. To some extent, I think José was covering his own assets—more guys finishing equaled a bigger payday for José and the team's budget. At the same time, I think José liked me and wanted me to develop as a racer.

I almost always rode in the car with José when traveling from a hotel to a race start or from a finish line to the hotel for the night. Jim van de Laer and Ronny van Holen were almost always in the boss's car too. We were the inner circle and enjoyed the camaraderie of that position. Conversations often moved from picking on the non-Belgian and non-Flemish teammates to cars, women, houses, and then back to racing. I was seemingly granted honorable Flemish status and forgiven for my American birth in the eyes of several teammates. At the time this was a unique honor;

there still were very few Americans racing in Europe. LeMond was seen as a godlike mutant, so his nationality was not much of a factor, and the 7-Eleven boys were still a mystery to the superstitious Europeans. I was nearly Belgian in many ways, and that made all the difference to my teammates.

I had been struggling in the early race season, fighting with my results and worrying too much about each pedal stroke. I had done well in the semiclassic G. P. Pino Cerami in my first two tries, so I hoped now for a result to open my season. The Pino Cerami race has the requisite large loop of the semiclassic followed by several finishing circuits in the 10-km range. On the finishing circuit was a short, steep "wall" that caused some panic among the riders but did little to shake the tree. The winner typically came from a small bunch sprint or a well-planned solo escape in the later circuits.

I went across to an escaping group on the wheel of Jesper Skibby in an effort that made every fiber of my being cry out in pain, anger, and fear. Skibby was built a lot like me, with a skinny, worthless upper body matched with a long set of legs with oversized calves. He was a fast, strong rider. As I fought to convince my legs and brain that it was important to stay with the Dane, Skibby looked back at me, never altering his pace.

"Ay. You gonna fahking ride or what, man?" he accused in sing-song Danish-accented English.

It was a rhetorical question, a way to punish me more than he was already doing. It was a good thing too because I was unable to answer and equally unable to come around him to take over any of the work. Surprisingly, he slowed down just before we made contact with the breakaway, and I brought us the rest of the way. I never figured out if he was done or simply wanted to make sure I offered up something to the effort.

We were the last two to make it across, and the peloton behind us slowed. Our break contained at least one member of each team in the race, and thus protected, we were quickly clear by several minutes. Frank Hoste was my teammate in the breakaway, but he didn't look so good. Team cars began to show their presence, including ours. José wanted to talk to me, but not to Hoste.

"You must make sure you go when they go," he said. "This group will not stay together."

I was looking for support from my veteran teammate. As it turned out, I was looking for too much. As I watched Hoste for some sign of leadership, the breakaway became animated and broke in half. The break was good; it picked up speed and motored away. The problem was that there were two purple-and-yellow IOC-Tulip jerseys in the back half of the split.

I was speechless and angry and frustrated and scared. I wasn't riding particularly well that day, but I was certainly more than good enough to be in that front group. I beat myself up for missing the split. Hoste and I each tried a couple of times to get a chase going, but each attempt was shut down by teammates of riders who had made it into the winning group.

And then José showed up again. He pulled up next to me, pushing me toward the side of the road, separating me from the rest of the guys in my group. I thought for a minute he might run me into the ditch, but he stopped well short.

"Y-y-you want to-to-to g-go home?" he accused, his voice an enraged stammer. "I g-go home." He rolled up the window and drove off. I believed he would not be there when I made it to the finish.

I limped across the line in 11th or 19th place, or something like that, and found my way to the café where we were to change before the ride home. I was a bit surprised to find José's car still there. I did my best to sneak through the café into the back room.

José gave me enough time to wash my face and get my pants on before he attacked, lashing out in a barrage of angry Flemish designed to scare and motivate me. What José did not know was that I had already punished myself worse than he ever could, so the loud lecture did nothing it was designed to do. Before he could give me the brunt of it, I saw his expression change. He had, all at once, figured me out. He stopped midsentence and walked away. From that time on I would see the man yell at, gesture at, and verbally abuse other riders, even superstars, but that was the last time he ever even raised his voice in my direction.

A few days later I found myself in the backseat of José's car again, and he offered the advice that shaped the rest of my career. He aimed his comments not at me but at the great Fons de Wolf, who was in the passenger seat.

"That one there," he began. "I have never worked with anyone more professional. He has plenty of character, but unless there's an argument in the peloton, he'll never win a race. Still, I would take him anywhere. If he could just understand that he could be a great helper, he would be a good racer."

That was all it took. Suddenly I understood my purpose in the world of cycling. José was giving me permission to be a good cyclist without having to win.

8

Controlling the Race

IN 1990 I GOT TO RACE A LOT. JOSÉ'S CONTACTS COMBINED WITH the résumés of Fons de Wolf, Frank Hoste, and Ronny van Holen had us hitting small stage races in France and Italy with the occasional trip to Spain. I was constantly on the go and was quickly finding out that I was one of the rare racers who become better with more racing.

We went to the Tour de l'Oise with all of our heavy hitters plus our token Waal, 23-year-old Patrice Bar. Patrice was not a bad rider, but he was from Wallonia, the French-speaking part of Belgium, and was therefore a second-class citizen in the eyes of some of his teammates. As an American, I was almost less a foreigner than Patrice, a countryman.

On the first stage of the race we were going to set up Gino de Backer for the sprint because Gino seemed to be the best guy for the job and José was becoming tired of having nothing in the win column. Everyone pitched in to take Gino to the line—everyone, that is, but Patrice. As a first-year pro, he was still operating under the assumption that his results were greater in the eyes of God and José than the results of the team. He hid out, whimpered when asked to help, and in the end pulled off a fourth-place finish. He was given the white jersey as the best young rider. The young Waal was ecstatic, but the old guard was pissed.

Stage two was a 42-km team time trial that would have absolutely no bearing on the general classification unless a rider got dropped from the rest of his team. In other words, the whole team could do the race at a leisurely cyclotourist pace and lose nothing, even if those riders finished two hours behind everyone else. If one of the team's riders fell behind that group, though, he would be penalized the entire amount of time he finished behind the winning team. My only other experience with team time trials had come almost three years earlier, when I was a squeaky-clean new pro with the TVM team in Burgos, so I was a little nervous about it. The rest of the guys were still busy being mad at Patrice and planned to punish him for his lack of help in stage 1.

It is said that revenge is a dish best served cold. I would offer that revenge, when served *in* the cold, by a bunch of lunatic old Belgian pros, is absolutely hilarious. We were all clued in to Patrice's punishment before the start. We were to let him keep his nose out in the wind longer than he should for a team time trial. The rest of us would then overtake him en masse, causing a gap between him and the back of our group. He would have to close that gap to benefit from any possible draft. But as soon as he made contact with the back of our group and had a chance to breathe, we would all rush through the line, leaving him to flounder for another long stretch in front. A good team time trial rotation moves like the track of a military tank. Ours moved with the precision of a clown-bike wheel.

The funny part was that we were actually going a hell of a lot harder than we would have if we had been going for the win. What nobody reckoned on, though, was the fact that Patrice was wearing the first category leader's jersey of his career, and he was not about to give it up. His drive, determination, and greed ultimately did the rest of us in, and we collectively became bored with our mission at about the 15-km-to-go mark. He finished with us and was able to wear the white jersey to start the next stage.

All was not lost in the land of Belgian payback, however. Halfway through the next stage, I made it into an eight-man breakaway that took more than 10 minutes out of the rest of the field. I took the white jersey off the back of my teammate.

The fact that I was rewarded for being the best young rider was neither here nor there, as far as I was concerned. But having Daniel Mangeas announce my name on the podium as one of the jersey winners was one of the crowning achievements that defined success to me. To most Americans, the voice of Phil Liggett means cycling. To me, the voice of Daniel Mangeas will always mean cycling. Since my return to America, I have watched the Tour and other European races on television and have grown accustomed to Phil's voice and the excitement it carries, but the sound of Daniel Mangeas, the way he seems to add half a syllable to the end of each rider's name and each sentence, like a Southern preacher, renders me almost speechless. It transports me to the start of so many of my races in France and reminds me of my hope each time for a great result. This man has announced the names of countless greats. For that brief moment, as I stood on the podium, I felt like one of them.

I have to admit that wearing the leader's jersey motivated me in a way that I did not expect; I had not had the thing on my back for more than a minute when I decided I would go ahead and keep it. I even called upon Frank Hoste to help me stay at the front for the final sprint, to make sure I did not lose any time or places to my only competitor for that jersey.

"Okay, Joe, I will do this. But if I look back and you are not with me, I stop," he told me. The fact that a former Tour de France green-jersey winner would help me, a nonsprinter, stay in the front for the final sprint was all the motivation and courage I needed. The last 2 kilometers of this race scared me more than any others I have ever experienced, but I never let go of that wheel in front of me, and I did not lose that white jersey.

● ● ●

On the heels of a bunch of honorable results, José called and asked if I would like to ride in the Milk Race in England. Originally I had been scheduled to sit it out, though I don't know why; I had just gotten back from the Kika Classic in Austria, where I had ridden well, and more racing would keep my form up. So when the boss called, I packed my stuff and headed off.

I was happy to be on this team and hanging out with these guys despite the fact that the Milk Race was an amateur event open to a few pro teams. The Milk Race had a long history as one of the most difficult and prestigious stage races an amateur could hope to encounter. I was jaded enough at that point to look at it as another day in the office—maybe even a day at the office with beginners.

The morning after I arrived in England, we rode our bikes from the hotel to Land's End and looked out over the ocean. The wind was blowing hard and I bitched the whole time about how much I hated the wind and cold. Downtime is the absolute worst thing for a stage-racing cyclist because the body views that time as relief from the famine racing has imposed upon it and immediately starts to store up reserves and grow soft and stiff. It is rumored that the great Joop Zoetemelk would not even leave his bed during rest days on the Tour de France and would only allow himself a piece of toast to eat for the entire day. Other riders, such as Claude Criquielion, would put in six- to eight-hour training rides on rest days. With this relentless wind and cold, we were not going to be doing ourselves any good with a ride lasting longer than the planned two to three hours, and I was way past a piece of toast.

In 1990, when every beginning cyclist in the United States had a time trial bike complete with aerodynamic handlebars, there were few special time trial rigs to be seen in Europe. I felt fortunate to have a set of clip-on aero bars for the prologue, which had a layout that suited my skills completely. After a long, straight depart, there was a section of rolling false flat followed by a steep climb, a steep descent, and a short, gut-wrenching sprint to the finish line. I prerode the course several times so I would know how hard to hit each of the turns and with which gear to attack the short climb. By the time I finished my reconnaissance, I knew I had it figured out, and since I was going to be racing mostly with amateurs, I thought I had a chance for a good finish.

As the last guy from our team added to the start list, I was first from our team to start. I launched from the start platform with huge confidence and was on top of the gear immediately. When the road started to roll upward I was already prepared and kept the speed way up, around 50 kph. When I hit the steep hill, I gasped for air but kept the bike moving forward in what I thought was the right speed for the pitch of the road. I flowed over the top of the climb and rolled down to the finish in near-perfect fashion.

But there was a problem: All of my teammates bested my time. We might even have placed our whole team in the top ten or fifteen for that prologue—but my near-perfect ride was the slowest of our group. Our team had a standing bet for prologues in which the worst-placed guy on the team had to buy dessert for the rest of the team and the staff. I replayed the short time trial in my head dozens of times, trying to figure out where I had lost seconds. I tried to picture those guys going faster than I. I could understand Colin Sturgess beating me—he was the reigning professional world champion for the pursuit—but some of the other guys hadn't even warmed up. In fact Hoste told me he'd resigned himself to being the buyer that night.

The worst part was seeing Caynn Theakston in the yellow jersey of race leader. Caynn had been my roommate so far for this tour, and I didn't care for him much. He had come to the team with great promise and had supposedly won the Tour of Portugal or some such thing. He seemed more like a Muppet than a cyclist; in the hotel he was a mix of nervous energy, dishevelment, and proper English manners. He had a fair amount of contempt for Americans and let me know it whenever he had the chance. At one point he was coming into our room as I was going out to find out when I was scheduled to be on the massage table, and he got in my face about leaving the room light on. "You Americans are all the same." I didn't see how being American had anything to do with it. I was just running down the hall and would be back in less than a minute. If I had to turn the light on again when I returned, I'd probably be in the dark for thirty seconds while the stupid thing warmed up.

Our waitress at dinner that night looked like a slightly less athletic Gabriela Sabatini, the Argentinean tennis star of the day. Hoste and I had been calling her Gabriela from the first meal in the hotel's restaurant. She was either too shy or too put off by us to enjoy the compliment. My only consolation for losing the bet was being able to order a huge round of desserts for the table from her. Hoste was sure that when "Gabriela" saw how generous I was with my teammates, she would want to run straight back to my room with me. It was an interesting thought, but about as likely as when he told me he was going to become a professional golfer after retiring from life as a cyclist, based on the fact that he was able to beat his wife and kids playing miniature golf.

"Hoste," I said, "even if 'Gabriela' came running to my room after she found out I was the team's loser, she would leave as soon as she saw that fucking Muppet sitting there in his underwear, picking at his toes."

By the next night I'd been reassigned to room with Hoste, never to be reunited with Theakston.

● ● ●

The next morning, while I was dejectedly sitting on the hood of our team car, José approached. Sensing that I was still puzzling over my big defeat in the prologue, he offered some consolation.

"You were very fast yesterday."

"Fast? I sucked."

"No, you were fast, but you were the first to go. Everyone else had a special advantage."

I saw Albert laughing.

"What do you mean?" I asked.

"Where you were going 55 kilometers per hour, the others were going 95," José explained.

"How is that possible?" My feeble brain was stumped.

Albert quickly held his arm out straight and giggled. It was instantly clear that my teammates had been pushed at various parts of the course that were not under the watchful eyes of the officials.

"Serious?" I asked, shooting a glance at José.

He simply smiled. I was too relieved to be pissed.

∘ ∘ ∘

None of us had yet begun counting the days to the end of the race when we heard the strange news of the death of our young teammate Patrice Bar. Jim van de Laer was the first to tell me. Just a few days before, Patrice and I had been sprinting to top-ten finishes in the Kika Classic, and now he was dead. I was told he'd died in his sleep, that he'd had a slow heart rate that had slowed even further when he was fatigued. Twenty-three-year-olds do not die like this, though. Patrice was almost exactly a month older than I, having been born on January 4, 1967. I was afraid to go to sleep for a month.

Earlier that year I had been approached by Dr. Ryckaert with a new drug that was supposed to have a great benefit for endurance athletes. He told me this drug, erythropoietin, or EPO, would help cure my anemia, the biggest problem I struggled with. I was ready to sign up immediately. With a few more red blood cells, I might finally be competitive, if not healthier overall. The problem was that the drug would cost more than a thousand dollars per month. I couldn't afford it, so I had to pass on the treatment.

As it turns out, my poverty probably saved my life. Riders from Belgium and Holland were dropping like flies during those years before science caught up with desire and doctors learned how to administer the drug properly. Deaths from EPO were mounting, and as the news of Patrice's death spread, he was lumped in with the rest of the dead early EPO users, at least as far as the press was concerned. I hadn't been close to Patrice, but slapping him with the doper label was, in my eyes, an undeserved slam. I don't honestly know whether he had been taking the drug or not. I do know that the police investigated Patrice's death thoroughly, and no indictments were made. Perhaps I am being willfully naive, but I still believe Patrice's unfortunate death was innocent.

● ● ●

We were pros racing with the world's best amateurs in the Milk Race, which was a strange proposition. The amateurs' attacks are short and sharp. They do little to fundamentally upset the balance of the race. They never put anyone in serious and prolonged difficulty, but they are annoying as hell and serve the sprinters' teams well because they tend to keep the race together, which is contrary to what attacks are intended to accomplish. With few exceptions, each attack in the pros is treated with the same resolve as a Major League Baseball player swinging for the fences in a home-run derby. There are no checked swings; the rider doesn't pedal three strokes and look back. Instead it is an all-or-nothing assault meant to kill weaker riders. We were having some mental difficulty with the flow of the race.

Several days later our highest-placed rider, Van de Laer, was penalized more than 4 minutes for peeing in public (along with a handful of other riders). The race organization felt that the spot the riders had chosen for their "sanitary stop" was too out in the open and that someone might have seen them. They recognized, of course, that no one *had* seen them, and no one had complained, but the riders were penalized nonetheless.

With this arbitrary ruling, we were officially out of the running for any decent overall classification result, so we made a deal with Britain's Banana/Raleigh team. We would go after stage wins with some help from them, and in turn we would help control the race so that Banana/Raleigh's Shane Sutton could hold his yellow jersey all the way to the finish. Although this was in no way the desired situation for our team, it was the first time I would be called upon to truly control a race.

Controlling a race takes place at the front, and there are two basic ways to get the job done. For single-day races, a rider like me is expected to be at the front from the very start, making sure his team is represented in any early breakaway. That rider will probably not do much work, if any, in the breakaway. For stage races, if the team is defending a leader's jersey, that rider will probably be asked to set tempo on the front of the peloton. He will set it just high enough to cause potential attackers to think twice as they are lulled into the relative comfort of his pace. If someone does attack, he'll simply jack the pace by a few kilometers per hour so that even if they do manage to get away, they won't take very much time.

After the prologue it rained every single day. I stopped trying to get the black spots from my jersey as I washed it each night in the bathtub. I was also finding my way into a crash each day. We joked at dinners that even if someone fell over on the left side of the road when I was on the right, somehow I would find my way into the pile. The rain and the crashing were getting old.

With only a few days left, I decided to forgo the boredom of the peloton and its requisite crashing and go out on my own for a day. After studying the race profile that morning, I picked the place for my attack. I'd go just after the first king-of-the-mountains sprint in the hope of creating a gap on the descent. This sort of thing is usually easier said than done, but I was riding well. I was sick of the rainy English countryside too, so I was determined to make it work. I prepared for the attack, keeping myself near the front of the group. As soon as the first of the king-of-the-mountains contestants sat up after their sprint, I jumped as hard as I could. The descent was wet and slippery. More than a few times on the narrow mountain road, I misjudged the effectiveness of my brakes and tires and slid wide through the turn, barely keeping my bike on the pavement. It wasn't until the bottom that I had a chance to look over my shoulder to judge my escape.

I was away and two riders had come with me. My partners in the breakaway were Danny Neskens, a Belgian pro from the La William team, and a British rider I didn't recognize who was a member of his National Amateur team. When it comes to long escape attempts, my goal is to create a comfortable gap first and share the work equally second. I did not ask them for any help but just kept riding as hard as I felt I should. I knew the guys from the Banana/Raleigh team would not object to this breakaway as long as it didn't gain enough time to put their leader's race in jeopardy.

Each time the motorcycle came back with a time board, it showed that we had gained a decent chunk of real estate between the peloton and ourselves. We had a gap of about 2.5 minutes when we arrived at the next king-of-the-mountains sprint. In polite bike racing circles, it is generally accepted that the rider who has done the lion's share of the work will not be challenged for any prime or intermediate sprint. As we reached the 200-meters-to-go sign, I became aware that the British member of our group was not about to follow those rules. He jumped clear and sprinted for the climber's points. My Belgian partner went with him, more as a knee-jerk reaction than a genuine desire to amass points, I think, because he looked back several times over the last meters to watch me fall farther behind.

I was getting dropped. My legs had been driving our little train as hard as they could for more than 15 km, with no help from the others, and they were now not up to the task of accelerating. After the line the duo slowed, and I quickly caught back up to them.

"Hey, what are you doing?" I asked the Brit, who stared straight ahead without acknowledging my question. "You can *have* the mountain points, just don't attack us like that."

I sat on for a while, letting the other two do most of the work, until I couldn't take it anymore and upped the tempo. We continued on, running out to a gap just shy of 5 minutes. We approached the next king-of-the-mountains sprint. I assumed that our British friend would tone it down a bit this time, knowing the points were his to have. I was surprised when he attacked again at the approach to the line, just as he had the first time. I was more rested this time, though, so I didn't lose more than 20 or 30 meters, but it was an effort I felt was completely wasted.

"*Bedankt ehhh,*" I thanked him sarcastically as I rolled through to the front to continue our long escape. I heard Neskens mutter something similar.

We approached the next-to-last king-of-the-mountains line, our gap about the same as it had been for the last many kilometers. This time the climb was long and shallow, and I could see the line from 2 km out. The second the British cyclist climbed out of his saddle to grab more points, I went as hard as I could, moving to the opposite side of the road. I kept my head down for what felt like at least a kilometer or two. Neskens was able to come with me, but the Brit was gone. There were now two Belgians, more or less, headed for the win. José immediately came up in the team car.

"You must lose this one. He is too fast for you."

"*Ja,*" I answered.

The kilometers clicked off, and our gap diminished as the riders in the peloton started thinking about racing for third. Neskens and I now shared the pace evenly, knowing that there were less than 20 km to go. There was a final climb—a steep little kicker—followed by 15 km of slightly downhill pavement into town for the finish. Everyone knew the script at that point. I was going to attack the hell out of my partner on this last climb and with any luck ride alone to the finish. The hill did not cooperate, though. It was too short, and my 10-meter gap at the top was not sufficient to break the will of the Belgian. José came back up so fast that he had to grab a handful of brakes in order to slow down without passing us.

"That's finished now," he said. "You must stop riding."

"Can't I buy it from him?" I pleaded. We had been riding on our own for about a hundred miles, after all.

"No. He will flick you."

So I parked myself firmly on Neskens's wheel and shrugged my shoulders. His director, Paul de Baeremaecker, came onto the scene as well, intent on talking with me instead of Neskens. Actually, it was more like screaming than talking, and despite my understanding of Flemish I could barely make out what he was trying to tell me. His rider attacked several more times while

De Baeremaecker was screaming, but since I was planted on his wheel, they accomplished nothing. At one point the Belgian director swerved his car at me as well, hoping perhaps that I would either crash or be scared enough to lose contact with his rider. I think it is exactly that old-school, cutthroat aspect of European cycling of that era that I liked the most, so his efforts merely served to energize me.

Neskens stopped racing too. With 5 km to go, and the peloton speeding along in full final mode just over 2 minutes behind us, we were going just fast enough to get to the finish by nightfall. No one along the road or in the race caravan could believe what they were seeing. The two antagonists had nearly come to a halt practically within sight of the finish line. The timekeeper on the motorcycle stopped updating his board because the gap was falling so quickly. We were just past the red kite signaling 1 km to go when we were swallowed up by the whole peloton. Adding insult to injury, I was called as the random pick for doping control.

o o o

The rain refused to let up, and the crashing continued as well. There were only 15 km to go the next day when several riders came off their bikes while crossing some off-camber train tracks. Predictably, I got sucked into the mix and hit the deck so hard that the down-tube-mounted shifters on my bike broke off, along with my saddle and one brake lever. Albert handed me my spare bike from the roof of our team car and pushed me on my way. The peloton was motivated for another big finish, however, so I accepted that I would be rolling in behind it by several minutes. When I arrived I was directed onto the small finishing circuits within the town and crossed the line a couple laps later. I was pointed toward a small street where our team car waited for me so I could collect my warm jacket and get directions to our hotel.

My soigneur Dirk and I were laughing about how many times I had found my way into a crash over the past days when I heard a voice from inside another car. I looked to my left to see the British national team coach just a few feet away, sitting in the right-hand driver's seat of their team car. His window was partially open. I thought he was talking to himself, but in fact he was talking to me.

"You're all the same," he ranted. "Fucking cunts. You pros are all fucking cunts."

I ignored him, thinking he had me mixed up with somebody else, but he continued spitting obscenities in my direction.

"Pardon me. Are you talking to me?" I asked.

"You're a bunch of fucking cunts," he barked. "You drop our rider and then you get caught. You're a bunch of fucking cunts."

My brain was still trying to process his argument, so my mouth did its own thinking.

"*What* are you talking about?" I rolled over and grabbed the doorframe of his car, one foot clipped to the pedal and one foot on the ground. I sat on the top tube of my bicycle. He cursed me some more while I figured out he was angry that I had dropped his rider the day before.

"Are you serious? We stopped riding with 15 kilometers to go. We . . ."

"I'm finished with you now," he interrupted. He jerked the car forward, taking my arm with it.

"No you are not finished. You are going to listen to me." I did not let go of the car. Something inside my brain exploded and I flew into a barely intelligible verbal tirade directed at him, the weather, the other riders in the race, and finally his homeland. While surely a bit scarier and more serious, given a laugh track and some black-and-white film, we could have had an episode of *I Love Lucy*. But before I could bring my Ricky Ricardo tirade all the way to the credits, I was grabbed from behind and pushed up against another vehicle.

"I'm going to have to arrest you," the bobby explained.

"For what?" I asked.

"You're creating a public nuisance. We cannot have that."

"I'm creating the public nuisance? What about him?" It was too late. The coach had driven off. The bobby was still holding me. Tomorrow's negative headline was flashing through my head. I was thinking about spending the night in a British jail cell dressed in wet race clothing. I found the situation terribly unfair. I had been doing nothing but trying to defend my position to that *asshole,* and now I was going to be punished.

Bike racers and fools are sometimes spared the negative consequences of being in the wrong place at the wrong time. Several of the race organizers had seen some of my ordeal and, fearing negative publicity, intervened on my behalf, sparing me the night's incarceration. In fact, they apologized to me for the confusion and freed me to go on my way.

I pedaled the mile and a half to our hotel for the night. It was a quaint little hotel, more American than British in style, that just happened to be housing a bunch of American old ladies. I was still riled up and was ready to spout my story of pain and suffering in the general direction of my teammates as soon as I found any of them. As I walked down the hallway toward my room, Ronny van Holen and Jim van de Laer ran past me; both were naked, and

142

Van Holen was calling his roommate "bitch." The proper ladies also occupying our hotel were surely devastated, so I was able to relax just a bit.

Finishing a long stage race leaves you with a strange feeling. It is kind of like finishing your senior year of high school—you're happy for finally being done with the drudgery, but at the same time you feel lost when you think about what you'll do tomorrow. Patrice Bar's death added an extra bit of confusion to my end-of-race dilemma. I had successfully skipped out on every funeral I had ever been expected to attend, but I knew this one would not allow me such a luxury.

Patrice's mom was a mess, a combination of heavy tranquilizers and grief dissolving her in a way I could not begin to imagine. His dad was a picture of stoicism, holding his wife upright and somehow holding himself together at the same time. I could not understand much of the Catholic funeral mass but tried my best to look as though I did. I am sure my teammates weren't following along much either because shortly after the start of the service we all spotted a church mouse and spent the rest of the funeral watching him dart back and forth, as if he believed he were getting away with something huge.

9

Mexican Connection

THE 1990 SEASON ROLLED ON, AND I WAS ABLE TO PICK UP RACE after race outside Belgium. I did not have to deal with many kermis races, although I was not dodging them on purpose. Instead I was hitting almost every stage race that José allowed me to do. At the end of the year, I went to the Tour of Ireland. I have no Irish heritage to speak of, yet Ireland enchanted me. I was anxious to get there and see it, even though I had heard we would be rained on every day.

The end of the season was well within sight, and many riders were content to let the race roll along at its own pace without forcing the situation much. There was still some great racing, but the pace during the early sections of each day's stage was calm. The Tour of Ireland was flowing like races used to unfold in Italy, with a slow, easygoing beginning, a gradual build throughout the stage, and a big, violent crescendo of fast racing at the end.

I happened across Greg LeMond early in the race as I was coming back from a "sanitary stop." The recent Tour de France winner was fighting with his bike and sweating way too much for the race temperature.

"It feels like we're going really fast," he told me. "Does it feel like we're going really fast?"

I looked back at my rear wheel to see what gear I was in.

"Ahhh, no, dude," I answered. I didn't know what to say. I had just come back from peeing on the side of the road and this time I had come back at my leisure as opposed to my typical panicked sprint to the front of the peloton to find out what I had missed.

"You don't look so good," I offered. "Haven't you been training? What have you been doing?"

Normally I would have held my tongue. I mean, this was my old teammate and he was cool and everything, but at the same time, this was *Greg LeMond*. I meant no disrespect, but the guy looked like death warmed over, and we were riding at a pace that would have dropped no one.

"I've been playing tennis," he told me.

"Yeah, well, I just got back from pissing and then I hung out in the cars and talked with José for a while. You'd better quit, man. I can't see that we're possibly going to be going any slower."

"Yeah."

He dropped out of the Tour of Ireland a little bit later.

○ ○ ○

Our IOC-Tulip team and the Histor/Sigma team were testing new tires for Wolber. This is the kind of stuff I have always enjoyed. When you are involved in equipment testing, it feels like you have some top-secret technology. Cyclists tend to discount road bike tire technology, citing the small contact patch and the fact that the rider is the engine. But good tires roll better, they make a big difference in cornering speed, and they give you the confidence you need to fly down the fastest mountain descents.

We were lucky with the good weather we were having, and Wolber's new tires worked flawlessly when the road was dry. We had good grip, and the flats we suffered were purely operator error or extremely bad luck. But then it began to rain. Riders from both test teams started getting flats en masse, and we were all having a hard time keeping the bikes from sliding. A few guys crashed as if the rug had been pulled out from under them. They were going in a straight line and suddenly, without warning, they were sliding across the ground, adding new scar tissue to their hips. Needless to say, the test was canceled at the end of the stage.

On the morning of the final stage, which would have a criteriumlike finish with some circuits in Dublin, a chain of hair salons was giving riders haircuts in front of the crowd as a promotion. For some reason Phil Anderson, Søren Lilholt, and I offered our heads up for the show. Phil and Søren both had long hair, and I was sporting a redneck-pleasing mullet. None of us wanted anything cut off, so the hairdressers did us up in French braids. It was hard to get even my well-seasoned Brancale leather helmet on over the braid. José thought I looked ridiculous but enjoyed the humor in it and dared me to attack from the gun.

"Yeah, right." I laughed.

The starter's pistol only served to wake everybody up and call them to the line. Today the peloton was determined to roll out even slower than normal for a late-season final stage. I took the opportunity to go back into the caravan and bother José and

147

Albert one more time with my pretty hairdo. Since we had no one in the top of the general classification, they were a ways back. When they got to me, they were both wearing shit-eating grins and drinking Franse *koffie* from a thermos.

"Hey, Joe, the whole peloton is asleep still because they were out too late," Albert said, laughing.

"It's true," José confirmed. "We came back at maybe 4 o'clock, and there were still many guys drinking."

"Really?" I asked.

"Hoh!" Albert cocked his head to the side, giving further emphasis to his remark. "Drunken."

"How many?" I asked.

"Half the peloton," he replied.

"Zeker," José affirmed. For sure.

"You guys are going to be bored back here all day? I should probably fuck with them, eh?"

Their eyes lit up. It seems that torturing drunks or hangover victims is another universal language.

I rode back to the front of the peloton, which was a giant, slow-moving block in the road. Its front line resembled a nineteenth-century skirmish line. I squirted through and rode off as hard as I could, to the collective "boos" of the tired peloton. I looked back to find PDM's Martin Early on my wheel and the peloton attempting an anemic chase.

Martin's teammate was leading the race, so he was obliged to sit on my wheel until we had a couple minutes' lead on the peloton. When he did ride, he was definitely soft-pedaling, but I was happy for the help. If we could stay away from the peloton, we could contest one of the slowest sprints the world would ever see. José checked in a couple times during our early escape and again when we had run out to just shy of 5 minutes' lead. He had been laughing and happy on his early visits, but now he looked angry.

"Raas is chasing," he said. "Keep riding—hard."

Jan Raas was the director of the Buckler team and had apparently ordered his riders to start chasing. It was a strange move because neither Early nor I had any shot at the overall lead. We would have to take more than 20 minutes out of the field before we became any threat to the general classification. It was also strange because Raas's team was not leading the race. If PDM had been chasing, it would have been a different story. Then there was the fact that Martin was still riding with me. If PDM had hired Buckler's services to chase us, Martin would have been informed of the chase and would have stopped sharing the work. I would find out later that the chase had nothing to do with the race— instead José and Raas were involved in a feud because José had "stolen" Raas's head soigneur, Fons van Heel.

By this time José had worked himself into a rabid lather and was visiting me every minute or so with updates. The show the directors' cars put on in cycling's days before director-to-rider radio communication was amazing. He was dropping back to monitor the peloton's progress as well as to see who was doing the work and then racing forward to me with a report.

"*God verdomme*, they are almost here," he barked. He moved the car so close to me that I could have hit the doorpost with my elbow if I'd felt like it.

José was so mad he was stuttering again. "When they-they take you, you must stay with them at the front. You must stay on the back—on the back of their line. If Van Hooydonk does anything, you m-m-must go with him. If they stop riding, you must attack again. Uh-understand?"

149

I did exactly as I was told, but the race was on its own course now. Without an enormous sprint in my legs, I was unable to exact any kind of revenge for my director. I had a finish that would land me on the second or third page of the results.

After the finish, I was promptly robbed of my race numbers, helmet, and Avocet computer by some local kids. It was the second computer I'd had ripped off during the Tour of Ireland, and a fine way to end the season.

○ ○ ○

Of the time I spent with sport directors, directeurs sportifs, team managers, or whatever you want to call them, my time with José de Cauwer was my favorite. He had the complete package. He was part dreamer, part psychologist, part strategist, and part mom. Most importantly for an American hopeful, he was all these things in Europe. When he offered me a contract to return to the new and improved Tulip team for 1991, I was absolutely over the moon. I had never before in my career been invited back to the party, and now José was telling me I would be on the first team. We were going to the Tour de France, and I was on the short list.

José called me a few days after I returned to Denver, where my parents were living at the time, and offered me the telephone number of Otto Jacome, Greg LeMond's soigneur. Otto was assembling a team for the Ruta Mexico. José wanted me to have a chance to do the race if I was interested. It was a good opportunity for me to see what I could do over a three-week period, he explained—the duration of one of the grand tours. In reality, it was more likely that most of the Belgians didn't want to head to Mexico in the winter to race for another three weeks, but I took it as a testament to José's faith in my ability as a bike racer. I called Otto straightaway.

Otto offered me a ride on the team that he was handling, which would be supporting Miguel Arroyo, a teammate of LeMond on the Z team. My East German teammate Olaf Jentzche would be my own connection to Europe. In addition, there would be three other Mexican riders. I was promised $2,500 in start money as well as reimbursement for plane fare and my cut of the prize money. Truth be told, I would have done it for the plane ticket alone. I told Otto I would gladly accept his offer and proceeded to make travel arrangements. The race was starting soon.

Arriving in Mexico for the first time was a lesson in culture shock far beyond the queasy feeling I always get when facing any sort of border crossing. I am genetically predisposed to a fear of government officials, which stems from my notion that somewhere in my ancestry there were moonshiners. Breaking a light sweat, I made it through customs and was picked up and taken to the hotel. I had flown into Monterrey, which was where the race was to start. I immediately fell in love with the local style of driving. There weren't any traffic lines painted on the roads, so people drove wherever they wanted. After several years in Europe, coming to a place that was even more relaxed than America was just the sort of vacation I needed.

Along with our team, some heavy hitters from Eastern Europe, and some similar talent from the United States, there was Raúl Alcalá's team. It was much like ours, a mix of European pros and Mexicans. Raúl's Europros—Acacio da Silva, Erich Maechler, and Harald Maier being the most notable—were higher on the food chain than Olaf and I. Raúl and his guys had ridden the Tour de France that year so were a little weary. Olaf and I had not been in

151

France in July, but we had each done our fair share of bike racing, so when Raúl asked me to work with his guys so that we pros could keep the race in check, I didn't have to think long before I agreed. For me, it was an honor to be placed on the same pedestal as da Silva and Maechler. These were the guys I aspired to be like; they were working-class heroes.

Racing this way in Mexico was also fun for more selfish reasons, as I had no real contract to answer to and no customized, amped-up car horn in my ear signifying a pissed-off team director approaching to tell me what to do. For these three weeks, despite riding for a completely different team, I felt like the main enforcer for the godfather himself. When Raúl grew tired of the incessant attacks of the Poles and Russians and Americans in the race, his guys and I would ramp up the tempo long enough and hard enough to deter any more imagination on the part of the instigators.

I am a product of the great American experiment and cannot claim a single pure, overarching heritage. I am a dog-pound mutt and proud of it. A minister purchased my great-great-grandmother just four generations back in my ancestry. As I understand it, she was a combination of Creek and Cherokee. I also inherited some gene that has allowed me to enjoy heat, humidity, and sunlight. My brother Jim and my Aunt Peggy Rose look like they came straight off the reservation. In other words, while the Europeans' skin was burning worse with each pedal stroke, I was just warming up—the chill was finally leaving my bones. Although I was feeling better each day, others were reaching the end of their ropes. The knowledge was empowering.

● ● ●

I do not remember the particular stage we were on, only that it was long and hot and the road seemed to go on in a straight line forever. A Polish national team rider wanted my spot in the line. I felt that his request was a bit unreasonable for the current pace and denied his nonverbal request simply by keeping my distance between me and the rider in front of me. He then tried to bully me out of the way, muttering something I could not understand. I did not move. He kept pushing me, his voice growing louder and louder. A European professional would have handled the situation differently, using a combination of words and sign language, and I probably would have let him in. But this guy came back again, spewing the full nastiness of his breath, which had been upset by several days of Mexican food. Before the rotten stench had a chance to dissipate, I backhanded him across the face so hard I thought my right hand had shattered.

I prepared myself for retaliation, but there was none. In the same way that your brain slows everything down when you are involved in a crash, I believe the brain also makes you braver just when you believe you might get your ass kicked. I spewed some proper American cuss words at him, pointed at my spot, and then rode off toward the front of the peloton, where I felt I belonged.

It was at that moment that my disdain for the old guard—the Eastern European, Eddie B., USCF, stinky, fat, amateurish cycling culture—defined itself to me. As a beginning bike racer, I had heard the grand tales of the Russians and East Germans and their dominance as international cyclists. I had raced in the States against students of the USCF's adopted Iron Curtain curmudgeon wisdom, led by Eddie B.—Edward Borysewicz, the Belorussian/Polish rider who became the head coach of the U.S. National team.

I was now some strange Belgian-American hybrid, and the more I learned about the European professional peloton, the more I hated the Soviet system's influence, which took the craft out of bike racing and turned it into nothing more than a war of horsepower. Upon rejoining the ranks at the front of the field, I felt justified when I heard Raúl yell at one of the would-be attackers: *"Pinche los Rusos cabrones!"* Fucking Russian bastards!

It is, more or less, my only Spanish vocabulary to date.

For the rest of the Tour of Mexico, I was fueled by just the right amounts of anger and confidence. Maechler was out, and I found myself riding alongside Acacio da Silva quite a bit. Although my team leader, Miguel Arroyo, sat directly behind Alcalá in the general classification and had by no means given up the fight for the win, it didn't seem likely that Raúl could lose. I was starting to think about the money. I was not yet counting my cut, but I was hoping Miguel would at least hang on to his second-place spot. Each day was a little more nerve-racking, like watching someone bowl a perfect game. For my part, all I could do was make sure the race was adequately controlled and that Miguel's nose stayed out of the wind whenever possible.

I had been rooming with my Tulip teammate Olaf for the entire race. Olaf had been one of the main guys on the East German national team during its heyday, but now, at 32, he was a bit past his prime, considering that after all those years he was merely a neopro. He wasn't adept at reading races and wasn't able to ride like a team member, but he was strong and didn't complain about anything. He also didn't seem to have many interests outside his job. I am not sure if this was a product of his upbringing within the East German sports system or just the way he was.

In the weeks we spent as teammates, I grew to appreciate some of the struggles and opportunities he had lived with as a cyclist within the communist system. As the Berlin Wall was coming down, many of the top dogs from East Germany and Russia moved west to ride for the professional trade teams. Olaf was one of them. The first time I met him he was wearing clothing that suggested he'd just come off the set of a Cold War spy movie set in the late 1960s. He was even wearing a fedora. I came to find that Olaf had left home at the age of 10 or 11 to be trained as a cyclist after physical and emotional testing indicated that he had some aptitude in the sport. He had been a full-time cyclist, more or less, since about the time I was born.

When he showed up in Mexico, Olaf had a full-sized suitcase entirely filled with bread, sausage, cookies, cheese, and other delicacies from the Jentzche household. He was also well-stocked with Underberg Bitters to help calm our stomachs after each Mexican dinner. Our time in Mexico would make for interesting theater: Two guys who are barely able to communicate with each other were suddenly thrown into a situation where they had to spend the next three weeks together in a place foreign to both of them. By the end of the race we had learned to communicate in a language that was foreign to everybody else, as if we were a new, strange form of twins.

With the clock ticking down on the race and our departure from Mexico looming on the horizon, Olaf and I started to get nervous about our money. Neither of us had been paid our start money. Neither of us had been reimbursed for the plane fare either. I was used to waiting for months before receiving prize money, but Olaf was not and was fit to be tied. At every opportunity, he approached Otto to ask for his cash. I tried to get him to calm down and promised I would stay in Mexico until we had received everything, but his concern for our money was starting to wear on me.

We reached Mexico City at the end of a point-to-point stage. There was just one race left, a 100-km circuit race, with a start/finish line in front of the capitol. It seemed as if the entire country had come out to see us. For the most part, last-day stages take care of themselves; so many riders are there to throw themselves into the racing that the speed naturally stays high. On the other hand, with high speeds and nervous riders, the chance for a big crash is always present, so these stages are a real grind if you have to protect and defend a teammate's overall position. It was my job now to look out for Miguel. At the high altitude and with well more than a hundred riders still racing, we finished the 100 km quickly, and I was able to herd Miguel to the finish in one piece. Raúl was the overall winner, and Miguel was second.

The spectators descended upon us like a tidal wave. I felt as if I were in a weird 1970s movie with swirling camera angles and epileptic editing. Old ladies were hugging and kissing me and trying to get me to drink strange-smelling booze out of giant plastic cups. They spoke to me, expecting that I could understand what they were saying. Over mumbling loudspeakers, I could hear Raúl's and Miguel's names being repeated over and over. I am usually claustrophobic in the middle of a large crowd, but this was different. Perhaps it was the combination of exhaustion, contentment, altitude, and pollution that had gotten me? Then, as quickly as they had swarmed us, they were gone. I looked around to find the rest of my team. They were gone too. Everyone was gone. I was straddling my bike in Mexico City's capitol square, all by myself, with absolutely no idea where my hotel was nor any idea what it was called. Uh-oh.

I started riding in circles, stopping every two or three laps to look around, as if that would change anything. I tried to decide if one of the million different streets looked like a good choice to lead me to a hotel I'd never gotten the name of. I can describe in detail most of the rooms in the hundreds of hotels I've slept in over the course of my career, but I can picture the outside of only one or two of them at best.

I scanned the area for a place to sit down. I thought I might as well make myself comfortable. Maybe Otto or someone would see I was missing and send a rescue party. An old Volkswagen van that I recognized from the race drove across the square. I sprinted over to it, hoping somehow to communicate my dilemma to whoever was riding inside. As luck would have it, the microbus was carrying journalists, English speakers, who agreed to let me ride with them to their hotel. It turned out to be my hotel too. I was saved.

Olaf and I were scheduled to fly out the next day. My Mexican squad mechanics and teammates wanted a night on the town, and Olaf and I were invited. I was never one for going out like this, but the guys had been really cool; turning down the offer would have been rude.

After completely destroying a bath towel trying to get the black grime from the polluted streets of Mexico City off my face and eating a small dinner, we all piled into a taxi and headed off for a club. I had visions of a dimly lit bar, furnished with quilted red vinyl and crushed velvet curtains. We would drink rounds of mescal, and someone would try to get either me or Olaf to eat the worm. I was close. My anticipation did not include the fat go-go dancer, and we were not treated to mescal or tequila. Instead a bottle of brandy was delivered along with glasses and a small bottle of Coke for each of us. It was the most disgusting thing I have ever tasted.

Otto promised that all of our money would be delivered to us at the airport. A half hour before Olaf's flight was set to depart, the money showed up. They had carried roughly $18,000 to us in a large envelope. They dumped the cash onto a standing table and split it up. I shoveled my split into an old Adidas gym bag as fast as I possibly could for fear somebody would run by and snatch my hard-earned dough before we could react. When the counting was finished, Olaf took his share in the envelope, told us he had to go, and headed through security. I thanked everyone in a combination of languages, shook everyone's hand two or three times, and watched them all leave. My flight was not for a few hours, so I walked around, looking for a better way to carry my money, scared that someone might have seen me shoveling it into the duffel bag.

I found a store that sold all kinds of concealment bags, everything from a bag designed to carry a gun to whatever else you might want to sneak out of Mexico. I bought a cotton bag that I figured would hold most of the cash. It was designed to hang from a strap around my neck and stay hidden beneath my shirt, kind of by my armpit. I promptly made my way to the bathroom and transferred as much money as the bag would hold. Along with larger and smaller bills, my stash was made up of more than three hundred twenty-dollar bills, so some of the cash had to stay in the gym bag. Despite the fact that I was doing nothing wrong, I still sweated the passage through U.S. Customs like a criminal.

10

Blue-Collar Racing

I WASN'T WITH MY FAMILY IN DENVER FOR LONG BEFORE I HAD TO get back to Belgium. After Patrice Bar's death, Dr. Ryckaert had ordered a massive series of tests to be performed on each member of the Tulip team.

Armchair cycling cynics have often argued that the doctors gave us those tests only to make sure we didn't die from too much EPO. Though our relationship was purely professional, I considered the doctor a friendly acquaintance and would argue that this round of testing was altruistic. I honestly believe he was scared to lose another patient, and that Patrice's death might have been avoided had he stopped cycling.

The tests were conducted at the University of Gent. We were sent to the university in small groups and spent an entire day being poked, prodded, and tested. We were then sent home with a portable device to record our heart activity and blood pressure for the next twenty-four hours.

I was pleased with our team's staff. I had known Dr. Ryckaert for some time. Dr. Eugene Janssen had been hired as the team's hematologist. Fons van Heel, the longtime head soigneur for Jan Raas's teams, had been hired as head soigneur. We also had a sports nutrition company, Born, as a sponsor. Along with drink mixes and bottles, they provided custom-made vitamins for each rider, based on each rider's specific needs as determined by semimonthly blood tests, which were mandatory. Although I secretly boycotted the vitamins because they upset my stomach, I was comforted by the fact that my health was being well looked after.

I'd returned to Belgium earlier than usual because I had been invited to ride a few cyclocross races with Adrie van der Poel and his brother Jacques. If I did well, I had a shot at the world championships. Adrie and Jacques were to be two of my new teammates on the expanded Tulip team. Many years earlier, I had seen a photo of Adrie in a magazine before I had even bought my first racing bike; at that time he was a young pro, campaigning the classics with the DAF Trucks team. José de Cauwer was one of his directors. I would be racing cyclocross in France with the Van der Poel brothers within a couple of weeks of returning to Belgium.

It was a great setup. Adrie was one of the international superstars of cyclocross and road racing and could command big start money. In addition, he had no problem getting starts for his brother and, now, me. The races Adrie arranged for me were in the north of France, within five to eight hours' drive from home. We would take three cars, two mechanics and one soigneur, which meant each of us would pay for the costs of one vehicle and one of the personnel. Jacques and I each brought two bikes; Adrie brought four or five. It was not an insignificant undertaking for just three guys to race for one hour, but the pay was good. After expenses, I was able to pocket roughly $250 per weekend.

I wasn't a great cyclocrosser, so I looked at the experience as a way to get better fitness and bike-handling skills. Most importantly, I was getting in with Adrie a bit, or I hoped I was. Cyclocross would never be my main focus, so I spent my energy training for my day job. But as an American, I had the opportunity to ride the Professional Cyclocross World Championship if I wanted to, so I called the U.S. Pro Cycling Federation (USPRO) and asked to be added to the list of entrants.

The Tulip team was already training for the upcoming season, with four- to six-hour sessions similar to what I had experienced with teams in the past—two columns of riders with each pair riding 10 minutes on the front before rotating to the back of the group. For the most part, this was a group of guys with much more talent than my previous teams had boasted, so the pace was high all day. Once in a while there would be a pair who wanted to test each other, and then the speed would soar.

I always tried to pair up with Allan Peiper. When the two of us were driving the pace on the front of the group, it was like a street fight. On more than one occasion we raised the already fast tempo by another 10 kph, grimly fighting with each other until we ended our stint on the mark. In most cases the pair that relieved us would sarcastically thank us for the exercise and then slow the pace to a more human level. The best part of training with Allan was that neither of us was trying to be the "training camp champ"; neither of us was trying to embarrass or harass the other. It was an honest struggle with a challenging opponent.

Allan and I were similar in our cycling upbringing. Both of us had moved to Belgium from our native countries at an early age. Allan too had lived with a Belgian family early in his life in the country. We had both done our best to assimilate into our adopted culture—Allan had even married a Belgian woman. And although the teams Allan rode for and his results were much more impressive than mine, we were similar riders. Both of us could ride hard when called upon, but at the end of the day we had more desire than natural ability. I heard José call each of us "the most professional rider I have ever worked with" at different times during my tenure with the team. I loved having Allan as a teammate and would dare call him a friend. He was, without a doubt, one of the most spiritual people I have ever met but was always searching for a new and better meaning to life, so he was a bit tortured. He was like the habitual gambler who is able to convince himself that he has finally gotten the hot tip that will actually mean something, only to lose once more. At the time, it seemed to me that Allan was gambling with his entire being and getting kicked in the gut again and again.

● ● ●

I finally bought my very own car in 1990. It's funny to think that, having grown up the son of a General Motors employee, I had not owned a car for six years. I got a deal on an Opel Corsa that had been owned by a house-call nurse. It was white and small and completely nondescript except for the "1.0" emblem on the trunk, which let everyone who could read know the dinky size of the engine I had to play with. When I left for Gieten, Holland, and the World Cyclocross Championships, my little car was still new to me, and I tried my best to figure out the fuel economy on the way. Unfortunately, I was unable to let go of my miles-per-gallon thinking for liters per 100 kilometers and gave up long before I made it to my destination.

I had never had to sign myself in to a major race before, especially not a world championship. When I found the race headquarters, I walked in and politely told the delegates that I was there for the race. I was already nervous for a race that would not take place for another two days. I was also nervous because I noticed I was late for the official sign-in. The guys had always been straight with me before, though, so I was hopeful they would give me my number and other information with no major hassles.

No such luck. The American delegate looked up and told me I was too late; I would not be able to race. I was stunned. If I had been a French rider, signing in late with a French delegate, there would have been no problem, not even a raised eyebrow. I would have breezed through without delay. But the American attitude was causing a problem, like two magnets with opposite polarity that will not stick together even though we were supposedly logical beings, united under the same flag and passport. Part of me would have been fine being shut down by one of the other delegates; I was a little nervous about throwing myself in with the world's best cyclocrossers anyway. But being shut down by my own dude was too much for me.

I looked past the American. "Am I too late?" I asked in my best Flemish-speaking American interpretation of Dutch. There were Dutch delegates present, and I thought I recognized a Belgian too.

They shrugged. What was a problem for the American official was not a concern to the rest of them. I presented my racing license. The process was laughable because we mostly recognized each other—everyone except the American.

Now that I was signed in, the American official handed me a USPRO skin suit. It had short sleeves. I suppose I should have known better than to think I would receive anything different, but I was still disappointed. The forecast was for cold temperatures on race day.

I was able to ride some laps of the course with Adrie to figure out lines and entry speeds for the different turns and obstacles. There was one high-speed section on a road where I could not seem to get the timing right to dismount for the wooden barriers. I was also having some trouble with a huge drop-off onto a beach section—we literally had to ride off the end of a dock and drop about three feet into the sand. The fitness was willing, but I was running terribly low on the skills it would take to race cyclocross with the best riders in the world. I comforted myself with the fact that my spare bike, one of Adrie's old Alan bikes, would be placed in the pit where he didn't have one of his spares. There were five pits, and each rider was allowed four spares, so I was helping out simply by taking the start.

There were white boxes painted on the asphalt starting line, which convinced me that each country would be called to a box. They had done that when I was running high school cross-country; each team got to occupy one box, so you'd put your best guys in the front and worst guys in the back. I hoped I would be able to lead Adrie down the opening straightaway and into the first turn, like a sprint.

Fons van Heel had arranged a room for me at the same hotel where the Dutch national team was staying. When I got there my Tulip gear had been delivered in a cheap, team-issue suitcase. There were seven or eight two-tone green bib shorts and jerseys, a "foam" jacket and vest, a cheesy tracksuit, two T-shirts, a polo shirt, and a pair of Carrera sunglasses. This was my starter kit for the season. Compared to what's available today, it was pure crap, but new clothing signifies the start of a new season and all of the hopes it embodies.

The amateurs raced on Saturday; we would race Sunday. Saturday brought rain and mud, and I watched the Swiss rider Thomas Frischknecht absolutely destroy the rest of the field. He was a true cyclocrosser: fluid on and off the bike. I started to feel self-conscious. When it comes to the distinction between amateur and professional, the lines in cyclocross have always been blurred more than on the road, but this guy didn't look like he was merely blurring lines. What he did looked masterful.

We woke on race day to miserable weather. It had changed from rainy and cool to absolute, bitter cold. For me, it might as well have been minus 400. I was frozen and could not get any warmth in my body. The skin suit did not fit very well, and my handful of safety pins didn't do a good job of keeping my arm warmers tucked under the sleeves. Fons had smeared some nuclear-hot embrocation cream onto my legs, but most of it was absorbed into my leg warmers and ceased to be effective when I pulled the leg warmers off. The USA jersey I had worn in Ronse in the World Professional Road Race Championship had been something like the giant S that Superman wore, but this ill-fitting USA skin suit had no magic in it whatsoever. I could not have felt more out of place had I been dressed as Clarabelle the Clown.

The boxes painted on the road turned out to have absolutely no purpose whatsoever. Another American, Kent Johnston, had laid claim to being USPRO cyclocross champion, so he was called up second to last, and I was the very last rider called to the line. I wasn't nervous, but I was shaking almost uncontrollably from the cold. The start was like that of many criteriums I have ridden in the United States. I had a moment to get clipped into the pedals while the riders in front of me did the same, and then the whole contingent of world champion hopefuls raced for the first turn. It did not take me more than a half-dozen pedal strokes to figure out I'd be of no use to Adrie. I was already too far back in the long line of riders. But in a strange stroke of luck, about half of the peloton crashed and formed a big pile on the ground going through the 180-degree left-hand turn that took us into the sand for the first time. I was suddenly in the top fifteen. Now I had to really keep my position and calculate everything. Every dismount and remount of the bicycle had to be good, even though I was not good at the craft.

The ground was frozen hard, and the speeds were high. Conditions like these were usually to my benefit as a nonspecialist cyclocrosser. In this case, however, the high-speed dismounts suited the specialists very well—I was fighting for every inch with nothing but fitness. With about 12 minutes to go and still in the top fifteen, I started thinking about the big drop-off into the sand a little bit too soon and crashed transitioning from a steep downhill to the flat part of the course that preceded the drop-off. It was by far the most idiotic crash of my career. It was as if I had tipped over, and when I hit the ground it was as if I was paralyzed. My shoulder and face hit the ground at nearly the same instant, and my body went slack. My legs, still connected to the bike, followed it up and over my back, stopping all forward movement when my back refused to bend backward any further.

If I had been riding around in the woods by myself, I would surely have lain there for another five minutes, asking myself what the hell had just happened. Unfortunately for me, the Eurovision television cameras were capturing every last slow-motion jiggle of my cheeks and broadcasting them to every television set in Europe. I got up and looked at the bike. I had bent the chainring and handlebars. I fiddled around with the chain for a minute but couldn't get it to stay on. At this point a mechanical forfeiture was a good-enough excuse. My pit was on the far side of the course. I slung the bike over my shoulder and walked back to the start/finish line to DNF. When I was on my way out of the hotel that evening, cyclocross great Hennie Stamsnijder, who had been calling the race for Dutch television, congratulated me on the nice crash.

● ● ●

I'd been approaching the new season at a fever pitch. My level of fitness was better than ever, and my level of intensity was that of a Vietnam War sniper who had been creeping up on the enemy for two days while moving only a few hundred yards. I made the lead team for preseason races in Spain. A rider in my role would not automatically be granted the spot I had gotten—I had to fight for the chance to race with these guys. The top players for the flat classics were in this group: Van der Poel, Van Holen, Peiper, and Peter Pieters. I was pretty happy with myself.

As soon as we started racing in the Ruta del Sol, though, my performance dropped sharply. We were working hard on getting ready for the classics, and I was starting to go stale. We would ride the stage and then pedal another hour and a half or so on the Spanish roads before climbing into cars for the ride to the hotel. Adrie would climb into the front seat and promptly murder an entire bag of potato chips. I was pleased to stay awake just enough to look like I was paying attention to what he said. Though my testosterone level was holding better than the previous year, I was starting to think something else might be wrong.

The Ruta del Sol ended without anything terrible happening, so we took a couple of days to train easy and prepare for more races. We were staying in a nice hotel that had great food. Huge pans of paella emerged from the kitchen at night. It was the greatest thing imaginable. I had long grown weary of shoe-sole beefsteak, white boiled potatoes, and green beans; the food they were serving in this place was actually flavorful. I was rooming with Allan, and we listened to Led Zeppelin every day when we got back to our room after our rides. I felt like I was recharging body and mind, perhaps even enough to get me through the rest of our trip in Spain.

We left in the morning on a longer ride, through the mountains and to the coast. It was a clear, crisp day, and I felt like riding. No one in our group felt like testing anyone else on the long climb out of town—we didn't need to. As we started down the descent, though, the story changed. Adrie was on the front and immediately upped the pace a tick. I was feeling like the boss man might need to learn that I was the fastest guy on the team when it came to going downhill. This was the perfect road for it too; narrow and fast.

I believe I passed Peiper first and then Rudy Rogiers, but it might have been the other way around. I set my eyes on Van der Poel after a handful of turns. I only needed to make one more pass. Just as I had him set up, we turned left, away from the mountain, and then right, back into the mountain. Adrie was using the centerline, and when I set up to pass, I had to swing into the other lane. The driver's eyes that I faced coming the other way became the size of watermelons, and I locked up the brakes. I was probably only doing 80 kph or so, and the truck was maybe doing half that, but there was no way either of us was going to be able to stop in time. I thought about going wide but didn't want to risk going off the cliff. I thought about trying to go right to miss him on the inside, but this might have meant low-siding the bike and sliding underneath the truck. Although he looked like he was prepared to stop, I was scared of getting run over. I tried to get the bike to slide as far to the right as I could but only got it as far as the truck's left headlight. My right brake lever and fist punched through the headlight, and I smashed into the grill before falling to the ground.

"Shit!" I yelled. I was back up on my feet before anyone else had even figured out what they were seeing. I think the poor truck driver was just about stroking out. When he finally stepped down from the truck, he was ghost-white and shaking. Peiper calmed him down, assuring him that I was okay. I laughed a bit, but I don't think he heard me. We gave him our hotel information in case he wanted to get some money from us for the damages to his truck. My bike was barely good enough to be ridden back to the hotel. My handlebars had been bent so that the left side was normal while the right side was now turned upward like the bike a Hennepin Avenue drunk would ride. I was so embarrassed that I argued with my teammates to just let me ride back by myself so they could continue their day. I shook the driver's hand, made every attempt to twist my face up enough so he would know I was sorry for molesting his truck, and got going on my ride of shame back to the hotel.

The day following any crash I ever had was like a full-blown case of the flu. Every inch of me would ache, my ears would burn, and I would alternate between hotter than hell and dripping with sweat and chilled to the core. This was no different. I was a mess. But since I was on the clock and occupying a very desirable position, I was sent packing to France to join the second-chair guys. Being on either of these squads would, in the past, have been more than good enough, but I had started the new season with the first-chair squad, and this was a fairly serious demotion.

I was stuck in a room with Michel Zanoli, the Dutch rider who had been racing on the Coors Light team in the United States but had now returned to Europe with a contract from José. Michel was a pretty good guy, but having the two of us in a room together was a scene from *The Twilight Zone*. Michel, the "European," was not at all interested in wearing the Euro-team tracksuit but rather wore jeans and a T-shirt, used copious amounts of hair product, and read cheap dime-store paperbacks like there was no tomorrow. I, the "American," was no longer comfortable out of my team tracksuit, and the only paper I ever held in my hands was either the race results or the odd *Life* magazine I managed to find.

The races I contested from then until May passed with the same clarity as a day after a bar-closing bender. I was merely a spectator, despite the fact that I had a number pinned to my back. I was not selected for any of the flat classics, and when it came time for the Ardennes classics I was too far out of form to contribute anything positive. A few days before Liège-Bastogne-Liège, I couldn't get out of bed.

I went to see Dr. Ryckaert. He decided that the mononucleosis I had been diagnosed with a few years earlier had come back to haunt me. He prescribed bed rest, which meant I would not get to start the Vuelta a España, which in those days was held in spring.

It was a crushing blow. I was dying to do one of the big tours, and this just put me further behind that goal.

The punishment of watching other people in a race you're supposed to be racing is cruel and unusual. Watching Liège was not the worst, since I was still feeling weak and worthless. The worst part was that we had no one doing anything spectacular at the front of the race. I did manage to catch a glimpse of a green jersey once or twice, but that was about it. Sitting on the couch, I was part of the problem, since I was not there to help out.

Watching my teammates in the Vuelta a España was much more tortuous. I could see the signs of warm weather through the television, while the Belgian weather outside my window was as dreary as ever. I was starting to feel stronger, but my form was nothing to write home about.

I got the call from our adjutant director, my former teammate Dirk Wayenberg, that I was going to be doing the Classic des Alpes. I laughed into the phone. Somehow I didn't see myself as the best pick right then for a race that had "Alps" in the title. After all, I was still recovering from whatever illness I had, and this ride through the Alps was going to have all of about two and a half meters of flat ground in it. Dropping a boss-man tone into his voice, Dirk let me know he didn't care what I thought about it—I was on the team.

At about the same time, José called to let me know our team was heading to America for the Core States U.S. Professional Championship in Philadelphia, news that was much more inspiring. I had wanted to do the race for several years. I knew I was probably not going to win or even have a shot at the U.S. championship, but I was happy to race back in the States with this team.

Getting ready for this race threw me into a whirlwind of preparation. I was training harder and racing as often as I could in the hope of finding some form in time for the trip. I was *bij*-training, meaning I was riding my bike to kermis races up to 65 km away, racing the 145-km race, and then riding back home. I pushed as hard as I was able, even though I knew it was a bit too late. I was still not finding the mental clarity that true race form brings. My chances of doing anything heroic were slim.

The Tulip team selection for the U.S. Pro Championship week consisted of Adrie van der Poel, Allan Peiper, Colin Sturgess, Ronny van Holen, Michel Zanoli, and me. Our hotel was extravagantly plush by our standards, and the food was dazzlingly plentiful. We rode just enough to loosen our legs after our arrival in America. We won one of the races that led up to the championship so handily that winning on Sunday seemed less like a contest and more a function of just showing up.

● ● ●

I was enjoying a massage from Fons when there was a knock on the door. It was Charlene, a high school girlfriend I'd seen for three short months before I graduated early and left Minnesota for Northern California. In our junior year chemistry class I'd had her as a lab partner. She had an interesting brain and a healthy amount of disrespect for our teacher, even though she could breeze through the work without any difficulty. In our senior year we saw each other more seriously. But since I was on the cross-country ski team and we both worked nearly full-time jobs, our dates were often nothing more than watching strange, late-night television on her living room couch, waiting for her mom to call it time for me to leave.

Every year after that, every year that she was in school and I was living in Europe, we made a point of getting together somewhere. For me it was a great escape from the world as I knew it. I wanted to take the normal world of a young person back to my nest of training and racing and resting my legs. But I knew that the lifestyle of a normal young person and professional cycling didn't mix very well. I didn't want to lose my way completely and always cut my visits short.

Knowing that Charlene was going to be in Philadelphia visiting her dad, I had spoken to her earlier in the day and given her my hotel information as well as my room number and Fons's room number just in case I was getting a massage. I was completely used to lying naked on a table, covered only by a hand towel worn like a diaper and talking with any number of different people ranging from other riders' wives to newspaper reporters. My body didn't belong to a person while it was being worked on; it was a machine being tuned up for further use. Her presence didn't bother me at all, but I think it bothered her.

"Should I come back?" she asked.

"No, no," I insisted. "Fons doesn't mind people in the room."

I introduced them, first in Dutch, since Fons spoke exactly zero words of English, then in English for Charlene.

"Is she a truck driver?" he asked. She was wearing a slim mid-length gray dress and knee-high black boots.

"No, she is a librarian," I answered.

"What?" Charlene asked.

"Fons likes your boots," I answered.

I wanted her to stay but knew she was feeling out of place, and Fons was not helping matters any. He was prolonging the massage by mysteriously finding new knots to torture in my back, even though he was never in the habit of working on my back. The visit was too brief, but she left anyway. Her family was waiting in the hotel lobby.

○ ○ ○

On Friday, Peiper started getting dressed to go riding a bit out of sync with our normal schedule.

"Gotta get ready for some TV thing," he said.

"What TV thing?"

"Oh, I don't know, some American TV director wants to get some footage of us riding," he explained.

"Ahh. Okay, I'll come with."

"I guess they don't want the whole team," he said.

"So who's going?"

"Me and Van Holen, Adrie, and I think Colin."

I puzzled over this for a moment. For Allan and Adrie to go made sense because Allan's race diaries had made him popular in English-speaking countries, and Adrie was a star. Van Holen's selection made sense too, since he had some bigger wins under his belt. Colin had been world champion in the pro pursuit, on the track, so I understood his inclusion. But one rider was missing.

"Hey, what about me?" I protested. "I'm a fucking American on a fucking European team! I mean, there's like *two* of us!"

"Yeah," Peiper chimed in, as if he'd just come up with a good idea. "You should be there too. I'll tell the director that they should have you along."

I got dressed and went to the lobby with Allan. But of course it was just a film crew—there was no one there who could make a decision to change anything.

"Fuck it," I said, in the general direction of my teammates, and rolled off on a ride by myself.

○ ○ ○

Race day finally arrived after what felt like a life sentence without parole. I'd never been particularly fond of the East Coast, but the boredom and frustration I felt over the course of a week in my own country sealed it. I just needed to get through this day and make it onto the flight back home, and then the world would be set right again. José had told me he was going to take me to the Tour de Suisse, and I was already looking forward to it. It was hotter than hell in downtown Philadelphia, so I rolled my jersey collar inside the neck and looked for a place in the shade to wait for the gun to go off.

When we finally got the signal to start racing, I felt as if I were punching a clock at the start of a twelve-hour shift that I'd tried to get out of, without success. I have started races pissed off before, sometimes with great success, but in this situation the anger had turned to apathy and I wanted the day to end. I knew Adrie was riding well and figured I should do whatever I could to make sure he stayed out of trouble. Peiper was finding about the same amount of enjoyment riding on the streets of Philadelphia as I and dropped out of the race after five or six of the big laps. Colin, who'd been floundering all season, found himself dropped on one of the circuit's sharp little climbs. Our six-man team had been reduced to three and a half: Adrie, Van Holen, and I riding reasonably well, and Zanoli as the half. Zanoli had been holed up in his hotel room the entire week and was now camped out at the very back of the peloton.

The Philadelphia racecourse was not a selective one; it was mostly flat, with one notable climb, the Manayunk Wall, and a couple of smaller hills closer to the city. After a bunch of long laps over the whole course, the race finished with a series of short circuits around the start/finish line, which gave the peloton plenty of time to regroup. It was a race that would be dictated by timing and luck, not terrain, which was frustrating; riding around in a nervous peloton waiting for something to happen did not help my frame of mind. If I had been riding better and thinking about some great result, my attitude might have been more positive, but as it was I found myself looking around for a reason to go to work.

Luckily, with a bit more than one big lap to go, a breakaway formed, saving us all from terminal boredom. The group was large, and many teams were represented, so it posed a real threat. I asked Adrie if he wanted the gap closed. When he nodded in the affirmative, I went to the front and raised the tempo just enough to let the peloton know we were going to take some initiative in the control of the race. When Van Holen joined me, we jacked up the tempo another notch. Once he got comfortable, we brought it up some more until we were confident we would take back the ground we had lost to the breakaway before we reached the Manayunk Wall.

Doing this chase with Van Holen became one more surreal event in a week I wanted to forget. The guy had won Het Volk and the junior world championships and a bunch of other notable races. He was capable of kicking the living hell out of you in a team time trial or breakaway. But get him in a two-man, do-or-die chase to take back stolen real estate, and he bogged down, barely turning the pedals. Nonetheless, we managed to chase down the group that had escaped, just at the turn to the Wall. We looked at each other and then shifted to our lowest gears and crept to the top of the climb, knowing that the day's mental and physical torture was finished. We made our way back to the area reserved for teams, got off our bikes, and watched as the finale unfolded.

As a teammate, there are two types of helpless. One is where you watch as the finale plays out, knowing you should be there, riding and helping your teammates. The other is when you know you did what you could but you still find yourself looking on. Van Holen and I were in the latter basket; Peiper was in the former. In a stage race we would still have been riding, but this was a one-day race, so we were watching. I am not sure which is harder, to tell you the truth. This was like watching a car crash with multiple fatalities. I wanted to shield my eyes but was eager to see the blood and guts at the same time.

I knew Adrie would be okay. He was the hardest-working and most resourceful cyclist I have ever known. I was not so sure he was up to winning the thing outright. But when Zanoli won, we were all rendered completely speechless. We had not seen it coming. What was worse was that none of us really wanted him to win, although the payday that came with it was okay by me.

I sat on the grass with José and Allan and Adrie. José gave Allan a bit of grief for dropping out of the race so early. He pointed to me, reminding my roommate that I had done work in what was supposed to have been my national championship. I had not been good enough to think about any national championship, but I did not correct José. Adrie, who'd finished fourth or fifth or something like that, had taken his socks off during the discussion. José grabbed them and threw them toward the street.

"Hey, America, these are Van der Poel's socks. You can have them!" he screamed.

o o o

I warmed up for the prologue of the Tour de Suisse in the streets of Basel. I had absolutely no delusions of winning anything; I just wanted to make it through this first test with as little pain as possible. I rolled around, looking at the buildings and watching the time so I would not come to the start line too late. I found Switzerland to be very interesting. I had already seen a bunch of heroin addicts lying on the steps of an old building. They were a great diversion from the prologue I was about to do.

Before leaving for Switzerland, I had heard Peiper say we had no chance of doing anything in this race, that it was too hard, and that nobody on the team was good enough at the time. I felt good that I was there at all. Most of the guys from Philadelphia had been left in Belgium, racing around the church tower in kermis races.

On stage 1, I got into a tangle with Michel Dernies, a French-speaking Belgian riding for the American Motorola team. Dernies had the amazing ability to make himself visible at the exact moment when the camera helicopter arrived. I was moving up to the front of the peloton on the left side of the road and approached a parked car. I was just passing Dernies when I needed to move to the right or become a hood ornament. I made a quick little gesture at him and moved over. The move was not dangerous or a breach of etiquette, but Michel took exception to it anyway and read me the riot act. He then passed me back and made an exaggerated move toward me, grabbing his brakes in the process. It was a stupid and dangerous move. If we had been in a full sprint and he'd wanted to brake-check me, I would have understood and maybe even respected him for it. Instead we were part of a giant peloton with fresh legs and the nervous energy that fills a race in its opening stages. Dernies's dramatic little display of power could easily have taken down half the peloton. A chorus of multilingual curses came from our section of the peloton, all directed at the Belgian, and I felt vindicated.

For the first few days in Switzerland, my severe lack of form was clearly displayed each night in the results. I was losing time every day to the leaders. The Tour de Suisse is not the easiest race in the world to ride, and in fact, many Tour de France hopefuls stay away from it, fearing its climbs are severe enough and stages long enough to hurt their chances in France. I was losing time even before we reached the real climbs, though, and sweating like a pig. Unexpectedly, on stage 2, my teammate Luc Roosen won the stage to take the race lead and put on the yellow jersey. My form was about to change overnight.

A yellow jersey has magical powers. The entire team becomes stronger as soon as that team has to defend it. For the first time all season, I had a defined purpose. My job was to control the race from the front of the peloton. That meant that for the time being, I was to go with any group that tried to break away. I was not trying to actually escape with them; I was trying only to keep the race together. If one or two guys got away, I would immediately start riding on the front of the field, towing it along at a comfortable speed, hoping it would be content with the free ride it was getting. A small group could have 4 or 5 minutes if it was no threat to the race lead. As soon as those riders bumped up against that 4-minute mark, though, I would up the tempo to match theirs so that things did not get out of hand.

There are very few flat roads in Switzerland, but the race did not become brutal until stage 6, which was the hardest stage—the queen's stage, as the Flemish call it. The start and finish were basically at sea level, but there were three major climbs we had to endure, each topping out at or above 9,000 feet. The little graphic of the course we got in the envelope with our numbers looked like an electrocardiogram chart. The stage was also long, officially close to 241 km.

In fact, it was longer than that. The Union Cycliste International (UCI), cycling's governing body, had imposed limits on the length of stage races to get rid of the monster stages of years past; stages could run no longer than 260 km (roughly 160 miles). The Tour de Suisse organizers found a loophole and reached the point-to-point distance they wanted by neutralizing 50 km at the start of the stage. Since we weren't racing at that point, the distance didn't count, even though we still had to pedal it at more than 32 kph. In other words, the stage was considerably longer than what the record books showed.

Our team was not bad, but this monster stage would be the best time for another team to take advantage of our weakness in the hills. If they could put us in difficulty before the first climb, we might lose one of our guys who was climbing well enough to help Roosen in the mountains. This was exactly what they tried. The race went crazy from the official start, with attack after attack.

Roosen was not riding at the front and missed a big split that had some serious contenders in it. I was already at the front and was forcing the pace to chase the break as best I could, along with Rudy Patry. The rest of the guys showed up in a hurry, and we began closing down the breakaway. We rode as hard as we were able, sprinting past each other as if we were in the last few kilometers of a race we were trying to win.

It took more than a few kilometers, but we caught the breakaway just as the road started upward onto the first major climb of the day. We weren't even 100 km into a 250-km stage, and it was clear that everything was going to split up here. The group that formed behind the race, the one that several of my teammates and I found ourselves joining, was at least a hundred riders strong. I was happy with that because with these numbers we would surely stay within the time limit.

The road kept climbing forever. Guys in our group were stopping along the road to fill their bottles with water running off the sides of the hills. I ate what I could and drank whenever possible but was still struggling even with the leisurely uphill pace. As we neared the top of the first climb, I noticed many of the riders starting to move themselves toward the front of the group, almost as if they were preparing for a king-of-the-mountains sprint. I didn't worry about it and crested the mountain about halfway through the group. Our pace down the long descent was amazing! The roads in Switzerland are smooth and well-designed, and they're banked like a racetrack. It was easy to go fast. Every time the road dropped downhill, our group took time out of the leaders.

I suffered through the next climb with this group and fought for a place near the front for the descent. When the road flattened out at the bottom I started to come apart. With 80-some km still to go before the finish, this was a bad thing. I also discovered that we were in the neighborhood of 20 minutes down on the leaders.

With one big climb still to go, this deficit was surely not going to shrink. I started doing the math in my head, trying to figure out how many minutes I had left to lose. I am no mathematician, but the sum I came up with did not look good.

The road pitched upward again, and I slid toward the back of the group, fighting to stay with it. I started to lose this grip just as we neared the final feed zone of the day. Fons was there, and I was able to get a musette bag from him. In my weakened state, the two water bottles, can of Coke, and various foil-wrapped food items were hard to fight with, but I took on everything anyway, swapping the bottles in the bag for what was already on the bike and shoving the rest in my jersey pockets.

I rode for a while before going at the food, hoping the rest of the guys would slow down a bit and eat. Perhaps they did, but the pace still felt hard. I opened the Coke and drank as much as I could. I was the last in the line, and there was no one to offer the rest to, so I tossed it on the side of the road. I reached into another pocket and grabbed some food. When you're fighting with the bike and the pace set by others, the only technique that works for unwrapping these things is to squeeze them in the general direction of your face and hope that at least some of the contents make it inside your mouth. I fought with a couple of the wrapped goodies before refocusing my stare on the back of the group. I fished my hand into my middle pocket, where I kept the course graphic, to try to figure out exactly where we were in relation to the last climb of the day. I was hoping for some sort of reprieve in the form of a descent before the mountain, but there was nothing like that on the card.

Just as we started the last climb, Fons rolled up in the second team car. He was done with the feed, and, like the rest of the soigneurs, he would be using the same roads we did to get to the finish line.

"How is it, boy?" he asked. He already knew the answer by my position on the bike.

"*Slecht, Fons,*" I answered without turning my head.

He opened a can of Coke and handed it to me. He then started pushing me a little, giving me a chance to drink some of it as well as giving my legs a little reprieve. When I'd finished what I could, I grabbed the doorpost of Fons's car. He brought the speed up a bit, and I slung myself off it as hard as I could. I was back with the group, but the day was far from over. We were about 5 km into a climb that was 50 km long and would get steeper at the top.

By the time we made it to within 10 km of the summit, our group had detonated into dozens of little pieces. Many of the riders had still been fresh when we had gotten to the mountain and were already several kilometers ahead of the stragglers. I was no longer in what one could consider a group, but there were still riders in my general vicinity. Within the 5-km-to-go mark, Jos Haex was able to swipe a bottle of beer from one of the many fans that were still dotting the side of the road. Jos laughed and swerved away from the fans, holding the bottle of beer high above his head like some sort of trophy before taking a drink. I secretly wanted some too but feared that as devoid of life-giving nutrients as my blood was, even a thimbleful of Jos's beer would make me fall asleep on my bike.

I went over the top of the mountain not far from Sean Yates. This was a great place to be because Sean was not only one of the fastest cyclists in the world on a mountain descent but one of the strongest time trial riders too. At the bottom of the long descent we would still have to pedal some 10 km of flat road, and the clock was ticking. Unfortunately, Sean got going a little bit faster over the top than I did, so I was stuck two bike lengths behind him for the entire drop to the bottom. My guess is that Sean was about 20 pounds heavier than I was. I sprinted to keep up, trying to get inside his slipstream, but could not close the little gap. I thought for sure he would take a breather once we hit the bottom, but with his big diesel engine warmed up, he just kept time trialing his way to the finish. I was only able to use him as a pacesetter, a giant metronome, and hung on to his tempo as long as I could. I crossed the line about a minute behind him and about 40 minutes behind the stage winner, but within the time cut.

○ ○ ○

Climbing the steps to my hotel room took a while. I had two roommates that night, both of whom had already showered and were ready to get their massages. I sat on the bed and worked at getting my shoes off. My gut was distended from the horrific recovery drink I had been handed at the finish, but I was still hungry. I fished through my pockets, pulling out everything in search of anything that was still good enough to eat. I removed squished little sandwiches and pastries from the foil wrap and gobbled what I could like a bulimic on a binge, but with the confused determination of a junkie right after a shot of heroin. My roommates had thrown their food into the trash can, which was what we typically did, since the food in our pockets was usually a mashed smear of glop after a race. I moved over to the trash can and attacked their castoffs.

I woke to the sound of Dr. Janssen's voice and his hand on my shoulder, trying to get me to wake up. I was still in my race clothing, lying on the floor amid a pile of foil wrappers from the food I'd pulled out of the trash.

"This is not so good," he said in a matter-of-fact tone. "I'll be right back."

He had been with us at the Tour de Suisse for a number of days and had been carefully monitoring our blood levels, checking them with a finger-prick first thing in the morning and then again after the stage.

He returned within minutes with a bottle of Intralipid and suggested it would be in my best interest to have an injection. He handed me the bottle so I could see it was exactly what he said it was and then explained that it would give me a boost of what was essentially fat. He explained that the best thing for my body at that point was this easily assimilated form of calories. He asked if I had any questions. I didn't, so he drew about 30 cc into a large needle and shot it into my arm.

The next morning we prepared for another long stage. The use of Intralipid was new in professional cycling, so we had no idea how my legs would react. I suited up early and, despite my body's protestations, went for a ride. I was staring down the barrel at another 257 km of racing, and I needed to know what I was going to feel like at the start. It was a flat stage, and all of the guys who were out of contention would be looking to be part of a long breakaway attempt. My legs felt fine, and I was surprised to be so fully recovered.

José told me to stay off the front for a while because he thought the race would control itself. I disagreed, but didn't mind hiding, so I did as I was told. The peloton did remain whole at the start, despite some breakaway attempts, but just shy of the 100-km mark a group of about sixteen riders went clear. I was at the back when it happened, talking with José. The group contained several riders who posed a serious threat to the jersey if we did not react.

I went to the front and began to set tempo. The wind was blowing hard, straight into my face, which was favorable for us since the riders in the breakaway would probably not want to kill themselves. I was using a fairly small gear by chase standards, a 53x16. The breakaway held steady, never getting farther away than a minute and 15 seconds or so. I assume they had some dissension in the ranks because I actually started to take a few seconds out of their lead.

Ludo Voeten, our team's business manager, had just arrived from Holland and was riding in the car. Ludo was no fan of mine, but the excitement of his first day in the leader's follow car apparently transcended his ill feelings. José came to the front at one point to yell some updates at me, and Ludo was screaming like a soccer hooligan, alternately banging his fist on the side of the car and waving it in the air.

"You're taking them back!" he screamed.

I didn't know whether to laugh or hide.

My teammates joined me, and we began to actively chase down the breakaway. I did what I could but was definitely not the strongest of our chase that day. We caught the breakaway and again assumed command of the race, everyone staying at or near the front. Rudy Patry and I continued the lion's share of the work, but everyone else was right there to jump in for a turn at the front from time to time.

I rode on the front until just inside 10 km to go, when the race heated up as the sprinters started thinking about stage wins. At this point I slid all the way to the back and stayed there until the finish at Lake Geneva. I had lost no time for the day and was pleased to be at the finish line with the rest of my teammates. Even so, I could hardly get off my bike or walk. I had survived another massive stage and dictated its tempo for more than half of it. Luc Roosen thanked me for my efforts and took my bike to give to the mechanic. We still had three stages left to go, but we had successfully put our mark on the race.

On the final stage, the race opened with a flurry of activity, with attacks coming at us like crazy. Patry and I held a fast tempo, chasing down all of the attacks. It was as though we had earned the right to be the first two riders on the road that day—as if we were the ones in charge. At one point we had raised the tempo so high that José came up and told us to calm it down. We grudgingly let some guys go, which probably hurt more than the physical pain we were inflicting upon ourselves.

The rest was anticlimactic. My teammate Luc Roosen won the Tour de Suisse after some fifty hours in the saddle. I was in the showers when he took the top step on the podium. The Tour de Suisse is no Tour de France, Giro d'Italia, or Vuelta a España, but it's at the very top of the list in the next tier of races. Helping a teammate win it stands as one of the proudest moments in my cycling career.

11

Chasing a Ride

WE LOST OUR TOUR DE FRANCE BID IN THE ELEVENTH HOUR, SO I asked José for permission to go back to the States and train for the month of July. I didn't want to get stuck racing kermis races for three weeks and lose the fitness I had achieved.

I boarded a plane in Brussels headed for Chicago and then Minneapolis to see friends for a week before I went to Denver to train in the mountains. The nice people at the airlines sat me smack-dab in the middle of an Up with People group. They were young and bubbling over with happiness and enthusiasm for spreading some kind of good word. I, on the other hand, now topping the scales at a whopping 145 pounds, had eyes so sunken in my head that you could hardly see them and was filled with all the bubbly enthusiasm of a bag of potatoes. People talked to me and around me, but it was as though I was coming out of anesthesia and couldn't fully grasp what they wanted me to know.

This week in Minneapolis was one of the best times of my life. I was away from the gray Belgian weather. I was away from the kermis racing scene. Most importantly, I was living the life of a normal young person instead of a professional bike racer. I went on easy four-hour rides every day, and rested. At night my friends and I were off to interesting dinners and then to the clubs to hear music and hang out. To them this was all normal, but to me it was amazing. I had been living the life of a monk for the past six years. In some ways I could scarcely believe this world existed.

I had been granted the furlough based on my desire to train in the mountains, however, and had to leave the party to head for Denver. I spent ten days at my parents' house, training five hours each day: Get up, eat a bowl of cereal, ride five hours, go home, and sleep until everyone came home. I alternated hard days and easy days but kept the course the same each day. I felt like I was closing in on real form.

I went back to Minneapolis for one more week before I had to head home. It was another seven blessed days of relaxation, with no schedules or stresses. I managed to chew through the last of the $4,000 that was my cut from the U.S. Pro Championship week.

The day I landed in Belgium, I entered a kermis race in Deinze and finished 14th, still half asleep. Afterward I was told I was going to the Wincanton Classic and the Kellogg's Tour of Britain. The Tour de France was now over, and I had no contract for the following year. Other riders on the team did, though, and riders outside our team had been signed as well. I was more than a little nervous.

My form in the Wincanton Classic was probably the best of my career, but it failed to yield any result. I sat easily at the front of the field all day, on the climbs and flats and side-wind sections alike. It didn't matter. With just half of one lap to go, there was a touch of wheels in front of me and I grabbed a handful of brakes. This was the first time I had ridden with the new Shimano STI brakes, which were considerably more powerful than what I was used to. I caused a huge crash that collected perhaps as many as thirty riders. I jumped back on the bike and set out to undo as much of the damage as I could. The first of my teammates I found was Luc Roosen.

"Come, Luc," I said, pausing for a second while he situated himself on my wheel. We made the left turn onto the main climb on the course. I was nearly dropping the Tour de Suisse winner. We caught Adrie's group shortly after the top of the climb. I yelled at Adrie to signal I was coming. Our groups eventually made it back to the front of the race, but just as we did, the winning breakaway was leaving the rest of the peloton behind.

∘ ∘ ∘

I was selected again for the G. P. de la Liberation, an 87.5-km team time trial that was part of the World Cup races. It would be only my third team time trial, so I was a little apprehensive, but since the other guys on the team were fairly similar to me in size and speed, I figured I would be okay. The team was to consist of six riders, but our original training sessions had seven: Adrie van der Poel, Allan Peiper, Ronny van Holen, Olaf Jentzche, Peter Pieters, Colin Sturgess, and I. After the first session, it was determined that Colin would upset the flow of the rotation, and he was the odd man out. It wasn't that he was slow—on the contrary, he was probably the quickest of us all, and that was a problem in such a long team time trial.

I trained hard, even getting together with Peiper to pace behind a derny along the canal road that runs from Gent to Oudenaarde. This was surely my best chance at seeing the podium of a World Cup event that year, even though we were considered outsiders at best. I figured it was also a good chance to get some much-sought-after Union Cycliste Internationale (UCI) points. In the forced-labor camp UCI president Hein Verbruggen had built, riders were valued based upon how many points they compiled. I did not have many, which was one of the reasons my contract had not yet been renewed.

On the day before the race, we reconnoitered the course and determined our order of rotation for the start, one that would not only allow each of us to be protected from the wind as much as possible but also ensure that the diesels among us never had to lift the tempo when it was their turn on the front. In other words, if I, as a diesel, had to hit the front after the guy in front of me had allowed our speed to slow, we would probably stay at that same speed until someone like Pieters could pick it back up. I was feeling pretty good and rotated through comfortably. The team was a little stiff as a whole, which worried me, but I was excited anyway. The way we were working together made it a completely new adventure.

On race day I received a bottle of some magical potion from Allan's private soigneur, Dirk Nachtergaele. I was to drink half of the bottle fifteen minutes before the start and the rest at the halfway mark. I was assured that nothing inside the bottle was on anyone's list of forbidden substances, so I kept it in my pocket for the start. Our bikes had been fitted with the special drink systems that triathletes had begun to use; they had a balloon-type bladder mounted under the back of the seat and a length of surgical tubing that ran along the top tube and connected at the handlebars. To drink, all I had to do was bite on the end of the tubing, which contained some sort of ball valve, and the pressurized drink would flow right into my mouth.

Peiper and I rode around for about an hour before we were supposed to start. Getting ready for a time trial is a lot like insomnia, when you toss and turn all night long, watching the clock, cursing it for not speeding up until fifteen minutes before you are scheduled to get out of bed, at which point you fall into the most blissful sleep of all time. I looked at my watch every ten seconds until almost exactly fifteen minutes before the start. Peiper and I rolled over to the team car with just ten minutes to go. We still had to change wheels, take off extra clothing, drink half the potion, sign in, and climb the launch podium for the start.

We climbed onto the start podium as a team and lined up in the same order as our rotation. It had been decided that Peter Pieters would take the first stint on the front, towing us out of town at a decent pace, allowing each other member of the team to get settled before the real work began. As I waited for the start clock to hit zero, my body trembled so hard I thought the nuts, bolts, and other things holding the platform together would be vibrated loose. Finally we were allowed to go, and the six of us rolled down the ramp. Pieters bobbled a little bit, and I found myself at the front quicker than he was, so I ramped up the pace to what I thought was correct and followed the few turns out of town and onto the big road. We were quickly well on top of our biggest gears. Our team seemed to be working well together. It hurt like hell, but we were absolutely flying.

As a morale booster, team directors will often downshift before they drive up beside their rider in a solo breakaway to make it seem as if the rider is going so fast that the car is working hard too. José was no exception, and whenever he approached, the Tulip Opel's engine was wound out and screaming.

At about the one-third mark, the wheels began to come off Olaf Jentzche. First he slowed the pace whenever he came to the front for his turn in the wind. Then he started to miss turns altogether. Even so, we were fourth fastest at the halfway mark. I thought Olaf might come around a bit with a rest on the long tailwind section after the start/finish line, but it didn't happen.

Van Holen was next to come apart. Ronny was smart enough to know that he should stick around for the finish, just in case someone else had bigger problems, so he stopped taking turns on the front. This left us with four riders to do all the work. I was pretty sure the Panasonic and Buckler teams were still riding at full strength. I had shared the rest of my little potion bottle with Olaf by José's order, but it didn't seem to help.

Right about the time Van Holen was running out of gas, I bit the tip of my drink-system tube, hoping to get a little bit of fluid. I guess I bit the valve too hard because the energy drink flow did not stop, and the entire contents of the bladder sprayed at my face and all over my glasses. I tried to stop it, biting at the end of the tube that waved in the wind we were creating and bounced with every small bump in the road. I must have looked like a dog fighting with the stream of water coming out of a garden hose.

Peiper and Pieters were definitely the strongest in our remaining group of four and could still pick up the pace quickly if it dropped. Adrie and I were fairly equal. At just under 10 km to go, Adrie flatted. We should have kept going, leaving him behind as a casualty, but he wanted the points. There were a few moments of dissension in our little group, amplified by race adrenaline, but we decided to wait. I was pissed. We were about to lose 10 seconds in the actual wheel change, another 5 to 10 getting back up to speed, and who knew how much caused simply by the disruption.

When we finally got going again, Olaf was immediately gone, unable to accelerate with us. Van Holen was still there, but as a passenger only. Adrie was crippled from having his legs come to a complete stop and then sprint back up to speed. Our closing kilometers were nowhere near as good as what we'd been doing even 10 km before. Even so, I hoped we would still be in the top 10 so I could pick up my share of the valuable UCI points.

We approached the 1-km-to-go kite, and I found myself coming to the front of the rotation. I hoped to be able to get in a quick turn on the front and then get back in the slipstream far enough before the finish line to stay in line. The rules stated that the clock would stop when the front wheel of the fourth rider crossed the finish line but that every rider who crossed the finish line with the team would receive points.

When I hit the front I made sure to keep the pace the same as it had been. I wasn't calculating distance but felt like I should be relieved. I kept riding. I was still on the front. If it had been a normal race, I would have swung off to the right or left, but that would have been really bad in this situation, so I kept riding. Finally Pieters came past me, kicking a little bit as if I were leading him out for a sprint. I sprinted for Van Holen's wheel as best I could. When we crossed the line, I was two or three feet behind him.

I thought for sure they'd give me the points. If this had been a stage race, my time would have been recorded as the same as my teammates'. I was wrong. Despite what I thought I had earned, I was awarded no points for my effort. We finished in seventh place. We were half a minute behind Motorola in sixth but 2.5 minutes behind the winning Buckler team.

Albert was livid. I was still catching my breath when he jumped on me.

"You are a stupid person," he snapped.

"Yeah?" I taunted. "Why?"

"You are a goddamned stupid person," he continued. "Did you forget about the points, or do you just not care?"

"What was I supposed to do, eh? Flick the team for some points?"

Neither of us was going to win the argument. Albert was sincere in his care and concern for my career, but I was not about to start racing for points. There were already a bunch of those guys around the peloton, riders who would hide out all day long in an effort to secure 15th place and a handful of points rather than lay anything on the line for the chance to actually win something.

○ ○ ○

It was now nearly October, and I still had no contract for the coming year. Albert's wife, Rita, who had not approved of me since my arrival in Belgium, was now letting me know it. To Rita, I was the little devil on her husband's shoulder, calling him back to bike racing. If she could just get rid of me, then her husband would go back to his former life as a truck driver. In Rita's mind, a job in bike racing was not a real job but an excuse to leave her behind with all of the drunks in their café who came in too early and stayed too late. It was an excuse to stay in hotels and eat large meals and ride around in the back of a car all day doing nothing. I was no longer comfortable hanging around the Claeys' house and made myself as scarce as possible, often leaving to go on training rides before anyone else woke up.

I wanted to continue riding for José de Cauwer, but it seemed the team was now full, at least as far as salaries were concerned. I called Och about riding for the Motorola squad. We talked several times, but in the end there was no room for me there either. I called the business manager of the Festina team. He told me I should have called earlier, that he would have found me a spot. I called Dr. van Mol, who had offered me a spot on the Italian Del Tongo team halfway through my first year in Belgium. He gave me the same story—I was too late.

Peiper told me that he, José, Adrie, and Luc had spoken about kicking in enough money to pay for my minimum wage so I could keep my spot on the team. It was a flattering thought, even though they eventually decided against it.

The stellar form I had cultivated in June and July was fading. I had raced a few too many flat races lately. Still, I kept hitting kermis race after kermis race, hoping to finally win one, or at least make some money trying. Albert took the day off from working on wheels and tires and came out to watch one. I got into the winning breakaway without too much difficulty and did more than my fair share of the work to ensure that we stayed away. This was just another kermis race and wasn't even close to my home, but I wanted to win it in the worst way. Two laps from the finish, my former teammate Patrick Schoovaerts came through the group announcing his intention to win.

"I'll give five," he said to each of the seven other riders in the breakaway, meaning 5,000 Belgian francs per rider—roughly $125.

"I'll give six," I told him when he came through again, looking for acceptance for the offer.

He countered with seven. I raised the ante to eight.

"Eight," he said. "That's a lot. Congratulations."

I went through the line just like he had, telling each rider the amount and then coming through again for some sign that they were willing to let me escape their group a few kilometers before the finish. One by one they nodded their approval until I got to Frank van den Abeele from the Lotto team. He gave no acknowledgment of my offer. I came through and tried again. Again he did not answer. I stayed with him for another minute.

"Frank," I pleaded, "what is it, man? Not enough? Everyone else is okay. This is not a team race for you." Oftentimes we would be under strict orders to accept no deals if we were there with a team.

He rocked his head a little but otherwise offered me nothing. We kept riding.

"I will keep it quiet," I told him as I came through again.

I did not know how to proceed. I was fully prepared to shell out close to $2,000 so that the seven other guys I was riding with would give me a second or two before they reacted to my attack to try to win the race. Six of the seven riders were willing to take my money. The rider in the group whom I considered more a peer than any of the others would not even talk to me.

I opted for caution and attacked 3 km from the line, as hard as I possibly could. After several seconds I peeked under my shoulder to see a Lotto rider chasing me. Shit. I hoped it was just his way of making it look as if he had not taken any money. Maybe he'd gotten into trouble with his team for selling a race he wasn't supposed to sell. I slowed a bit to let him catch me. One of the other riders resumed a steady pace on the front. As soon as Frank looked away, I jumped again, as hard as my legs would go. Again he chased. I timed it wrong. I was now a carrot on a stick for everyone else in the breakaway and, with just under a kilometer to go, didn't have enough distance to hold off the sprint that Frank was leading out. It was checkmate, with me as the loser. I slowed again, hoping some strange luck might come somehow.

On the line, Frank was fourth, with me coming in somewhere after that. I rode up to him. What I wanted to do was climb off my bike, knock this stupid Belgian to the ground, and stomp his head in with the carbon-fiber sole of my shoe, but exhausted frustration trumped rage.

"Did I do something against you?" I asked calmly. He didn't answer.

● ● ●

Albert didn't come home that night. He still had not returned when I got up the next morning. I went for a one-hour bike ride through the woods to loosen up my legs. When I got back I saw that his car was there, meaning he had come home. Usually Rita would yell at him all day when he stayed out all night, so I was cautious as I walked into the house. I was relieved to find no one else up, so I sat down at the kitchen table to have another cup of coffee. A few minutes later, the shit hit the fan, but instead of Rita yelling at Albert, Albert was yelling at José through the telephone.

"You're all thieves and liars!" he screamed over and over. "You're all assholes!"

He went on to tell José that he was quitting, that they had one day to clear everything out of his workshop and that he wanted to be paid what he was owed, in cash, when they arrived. After slamming down the phone, he went back to bed.

● ● ●

After one more unsuccessful attempt at getting a big result for the season, I flew back from Montreal and returned to the Claeys' house. Rita seemed happier now that Albert was driving trucks again. Albert was calm too, but to me, it felt more like the kind of calm that comes after defeat than the calm of clarity.

I wanted to go back to the States, and since my racing season was over if I wanted it to be, José had no objections. I went to a kermis race to meet up with the team's new crew of mechanics and got a fresh set of wheels to take back to America. I had signed a paper when I'd received my bike that year that allowed the team to keep something like $250 of my final paycheck if I wanted to keep my bike. I figured a new set of wheels should come with the deal. No one objected.

"I hope to see you next year," José told me, holding out his hand.

"You'll see me again, José," I told him, shaking his hand.

● ● ●

My soigneur, Dirk, agreed to give me a ride to the airport. I got up a little earlier than usual and made coffee. Albert was going to be heading out with his truck, and I wanted to see him off before climbing on the plane for America. He drank coffee and dipped Speculaas cookies, as usual, and then got up to leave.

"Until next year, Joe," he said, pushing open the screen door.

"Yeah," I answered. "See ya."

Epilogue

I SAID GOODBYE TO FLANDERS KNOWING THAT I MIGHT NEVER GO back. I never did. I lost contact with my adopted family and most of the people who had so deeply influenced me. Maybe that makes me a horrible person, or maybe it makes me lucky. None of these people have grown old in my mind, or any less fascinating than they were when I lived with them.

For several years after returning to America, I was unable to watch a Belgian spring classic without a strange lump forming in my throat. I died a little bit watching my Tulip teammates in the Tour de France in 1992.

After the years in Europe, racing road bikes in the United States didn't really do it for me. I was never—not once—able to rise to the level of dedication I had mustered each day in Europe. A switch to mountain bikes in 1995 breathed a few more years into my career and granted me a few more trips to Europe to race. In fact, arriving in the French part of Belgium for the World Cup race in Houffalize felt exactly like coming home. At that point in my life, I had lived in Belgium for more years than anywhere else. It *was* home.

Never having raced the Tour de France remains a disappointment, mostly because I always have to explain why that section of my résumé is missing. It is not the easiest thing to explain to a casual cycling fan in the United States. Whenever I'm given the chance, though, I will try to describe the other races: the flat, rainy, windy, and cold trips into hell. And I smile when I tell the stories because my body has long since forgotten the pain I asked it to endure.

My souvenirs are a handful of photographs, two pieces of fan mail, one Tulip team riding jacket, and a trophy from my amateur days. The magazine articles and photographs of me can be counted on one hand. The money has long been spent. I worried about all that until Allan Peiper relayed a story. He told me that at some point during the 1992 season, the team dropped the ball during a stage of some race somewhere. José was angry with the guys and was giving them a bit of "what for" at the dinner table. José liked to do that. According to Peiper's story, José stared at the team and berated them for not keeping control of the race.

"What I needed today was my American, Joe," he said, "because that one could ride hard."

And that is enough for me.

Team History

Europe

1986: Amateur (Belgium)

1987: Transvemij/Van Schilt
(Holland)
Director: Jules de Wever

1988: Eurotop Keukens (Belgium)
Director: Florent van
Vaerenberg

1989: ADR/HUMO (Belgium)
Director: Patrick Versluys

1990: ADR/IOC/Tulip Computers
(Belgium)
Director: José de Cauwer

1991: Tulip Computers (Belgium)
Director: José de Cauwer

USA Road

1992–1993: Scott/Bikyle
(USA)
Director: Kyle Schmeer

1994: Coors Light Cycling
(USA)
Director: Len Pettyjohn

USA Mountain Bike

1995–1996: Diamondback
Racing (USA)
Director: Keith Ketterer

1997: Nautilus Nutritionals/
Barracuda (USA)
Director: Charles Aaron

Acknowledgments

Sky Yaeger, Steve Tack, Leo Sternbach, Jen Soulé, Pat Sorenson, Kyle Schmeer, Steve Satern, Bob Roll, Mike Riemer, Len Pettyjohn, Jim and Jay Parkin, Gene and Jennifer Oberpriller, Booker Noe, Tim Mulrooney, Charlene Lowe, Juliette Lewis, Mike Larson, Janis LaDouceur, Stevil Kinevil, Keith Ketterer, Nell Hurley, Michael Herbert, Eric Hawkins, Hansen Gregory, Peter Gilbert, Dan Fox, Jim and Scott Flanders, Gary Crandall, Coach, Kelli Castelli, Elayna Caldwell, Albert Blanton, Will Ashford, and Charles Aaron . . .

Thank you.

I'd also like to say a very special thank-you to the fine folks at VeloPress for the encouragement and opportunity to make this book happen.

About the Author

Joe Parkin represented the United States at the World Professional Road Cycling Championships and the World Cyclocross Championships. Following his road racing years in Belgium, he returned to the United States, began a successful second career as a pro mountain bike racer, and carried the stars and stripes at the World Professional Mountain Bike Championships.